Trade Secrets for Nonprofit Managers

WILEY NONPROFIT LAW, FINANCE, AND MANAGEMENT SERIES

The Art of Planned Giving: Understanding Donors and the Culture of Giving by Douglas E. White

Beyond Fund Raising: New Strategies for Nonprofit Investment and Innovation by Kay Grace

Budgeting for Not-for-Profit Organizations by David Maddox

Charity, Advocacy, and the Law by Bruce R. Hopkins

The Complete Guide to Fund Raising Management by Stanley Weinstein

The Complete Guide to Nonprofit Management by Smith, Bucklin & Associates

Critical Issues in Fund Raising edited by Dwight Burlingame

Developing Affordable Housing: A Practical Guide for Nonprofit Organizations, Second Edition by Bennett L. Hecht

Faith-Based Management: Leading Organizations that are Based on More than Just Mission by Peter Brinckerhoff

Financial and Accounting Guide for Not-for-Profit Organizations, Sixth Edition by Malvern J. Gross, Jr., Richard F. Larkin, Roger S. Bruttomesso, John J. McNally, PricewaterhouseCoopers LLP

Financial Empowerment: More Money for More Mission by Peter Brinckerhoff

Financial Management for Nonprofit Organizations by Jo Ann Hankin, Alan Seidner and John Zietlow

Financial Planning for Nonprofit Organizations by Jody Blazek

The First Legal Answer Book for Fund-Raisers by Bruce R. Hopkins

The Fund Raiser's Guide to the Internet by Michael Johnston

Fund-Raising: Evaluating and Managing the Fund Development Process, Second Edition by James M. Greenfield

Fund-Raising Fundamentals: A Guide to Annual Giving for Professionals and Volunteers by James M. Greenfield

Fundraising Cost Effectiveness: A Self-Assessment Workbook by James M. Greenfield

Fund-Raising Regulation: A State-by-State Handbook of Registration Forms, Requirements, and Procedures by Seth Perlman and Betsy Hills Bush

Grantseeker's Toolkit: A Comprehensive Guide to Finding Funding by Cheryl S. New and James A. Quick

Grant Winner's Toolkit: Project Management and Evaluation by James A. Quick and Cheryl S. New

High Performance Nonprofit Organizations: Managing Upstream for Greater Impact by Christine Letts, William Ryan, and Allen Grossman

Intermediate Sanctions: Curbing Nonprofit Abuse by Bruce R. Hopkins and D. Benson Tesdahl

Private Foundations: Tax Law and Compliance by Bruce R. Hopkins and Jody Blazek

Program Related Investments: A Technical Manual for Foundations by Christie I. Baxter.

Reengineering Your Nonprofit Organization: A Guide to Strategic Transformation by Alceste T. Pappas

Reinventing the University: Managing and Financing Institutions of Higher Education by Sandra L. Johnson and Sean C. Rush, PricewaterhouseCoopers LLP

The Second Legal Answer Book for Nonprofit Organizations by Bruce R. Hopkins

Social Entrepreneurship: The Art of Mission-Based Venture Development by Peter Brinckerhoff

Special Events: Proven Strategies for Nonprofit Fund Raising by Alan Wendroff

Strategic Communications for Nonprofit Organizations: Seven Steps to Creating a Successful Plan by Janel Radtke

Strategic Planning for Nonprofit Organizations: A Practical Guide and Workbook by Michael Allison and Jude Kaye, Support Center for Nonprofit Management

Streetsmart Financial Basics for Nonprofit Managers by Thomas A. McLaughlin

A Streetsmart Guide to Nonprofit Mergers and Networks by Thomas A. McLaughlin

Successful Marketing Strategies for Nonprofit Organizations by Barry J. McLeish

Successful Corporate Fund Raising: Effective Strategies for Today's Nonprofits by Scott Sheldon

The Tax Law of Charitable Giving, Second Edition by Bruce R. Hopkins

The Tax Law of Colleges and Universities by Bertrand M. Harding

Tax Planning and Compliance for Tax-Exempt Organizations: Forms, Checklists, Procedures, Third Edition by Jody Blazek

Trade Secrets for Every Nonprofit Manager by Thomas A. McLaughlin

The Universal Benefits of Volunteering: A Practical Workbook for Nonprofit Organizations, Volunteers and Corporations by Walter P. Pidgeon, Jr.

The Volunteer Management Handbook by Tracy Daniel Connors

Values-Based Estate Planning: A Step-by-Step Approach to Wealth Transfers for Professional Advisors by Scott Fithian

Trade Secrets for Nonprofit Managers

Thomas A. McLaughlin

John Wiley & Sons, Inc.

New York • Chichester • Weinheim • Brisbane • Singapore • Toronto

Library of Congress Cataloging-in-Publication Data:
McLaughlin, Thomas A.
    Trade secrets for nonprofit managers/Thomas A. McLaughlin.
        p. cm. — (Wiley nonprofit law, finance, and management series)
    ISBN 0-471-38952-8 (cloth : alk. paper)
    1. Nonprofit organizations—Management.   I. Title.   II. Series.
HD62.6 .M395 2001
658´.048—dc21   00-043380

Printed in the United States of America

10 9 8 7 6 5 4 3 2 1

To my parents,
Charles and Lucille,
who gave me the gift of opportunity.

Contents

Acknowledgments

This is a book about ideas, so many people will be able to see their fingerprints on it. Those who contributed ideas through their books and articles are far too numerous to mention. But to those who shaped my thinking through a sustained relationship of some kind, by offering an important insight or challenging my ideas, or who just made an offhand remark deserve specific recognition. They are the ones to whom I owe special recognition, because it is their influence that it is too pervasive to be captured in a single citation.

Yitzhak Bakal and Peter Nessen gave me the sustained opportunities that are the source of many of these ideas. Paul Clolery usually is the first to give voice to my thoughts. Marla Bobowick and Martha Cooley helped make this and my previous books into something worth publishing. Melissa Kahn and John Hopkins suggest, shape, and help refine this and similar material every day. And the following individuals provided or embodied many of the trade secrets I have tried to capture: Mike Brennan; Tom Brown; Peggy Charren; Leighton Cheney; Bob Cowden; Roseanne DiStephano; Geri Dorr; Jed Emerson; Kay Frishman; Bob Harris; Frances Hesselbein; Ann Hill; David Jordan; Carol Katz; Kathy Maul; Crys McCuin; John McManus; Peter Nessen; Regis Obijiski; Ginny Purcell; Gail Sendecke; Nancy Silver Hargreaves; Jack Stone; Bill Taylor; Sudhakar Vamethaven; Rick Walker.

Finally, I must thank my wife Gail Sendecke and my children, Paul and Emily, for allowing me the time to document and share these secrets with you.

Introduction

Within a few days of being hired, the average non-profit manager makes an unsettling discovery—everyone is too nice. People are on their best behavior when dealing with nonprofits. The general public—a category certain to include most of the manager's immediate and extended family, friends, neighbors, the consumer loan lady at the bank, and the mailman—regards nonprofits as *cute*. Politicians attend agency fundraisers and speak many fine words about many fine accomplishments. Academics marvel at the usefulness of these little organizations. Local business people can't say enough good things about how nonprofits enrich their community.

These are well-meaning behaviors from well-meaning people, but they carry a subtly heavy penalty for nonprofit organizations and their stakeholders. If something is cute, you don't need to take it seriously. The nonprofit manager who buys into this dynamic risks losing self-esteem and effectiveness.

When organizations and their managers are routinely patronized in this way, it becomes impossible to have an honest and effective dialog about their management. Business principles and practices begin to seem out of place. Board members may fear alienating the staff if they question choices made by management. Funders may simply look at superficial realities and accept assertions at face value, or they may quietly take their money elsewhere. Media outlets may either ignore nonprofits or play gotcha with a few unfortunate stragglers from the nonprofit pack.

For those connected with nonprofits, take heart. The sector is among the fastest growing in our economy. The number of nonprofit public charities is growing rapidly and is on track to exceed a mil-

1

lion within a few years. One in 25 workers in this country is an employee of a nonprofit organization, and the rate of increase in nonprofit employment exceeds that of government at all levels. Eventually, this sector will be accorded the respect it deserves. In the meantime, we need plenty of straight talk. We need to share trade secrets.

This book is designed to be a place where anyone connected with a nonprofit organization—funders, board members, managers, volunteers, academics, advisors, clients, and suppliers—can find forthright, practical information about nonprofit management. It is based on 25 years of nonprofit experience as a direct service worker, manager, board member, lobbyist, consultant, and instructor. It is intended to inform, educate, and, on occasion, entertain. Most of all, it is intended to challenge all those niceties and offer some ways to get things done.

Most of the pieces here were originally published in *The Nonprofit Times* and elsewhere. All were written with the practical realities of nonprofit managers and other nonprofit leaders in mind.

THE NONPROFIT MANAGEMENT FRAMEWORK

Let's begin with a framework. Figure 1 presents our model for nonprofit management. It illustrates the interplay between different elements of a nonprofit organization and provides a useful tool for analyzing and evaluating operations.

Notice the tentative connection between vision and mission. This connection is intentionally drawn with a dashed line to illustrate the inherently tentative nature of the relationship. Whereas mission, strategy, organizational structure, and resources are directly and consistently connected, vision has less distinct relationship with other elements in the nonprofit management framework.

Vision is the dream which provides the impetus for all operations of an organization. Often, vision exists in the mind and heart of an organization's founder, and is most important at the beginning of an organization's development, and at key junctures thereafter. Vision is such an inherently personal notion that it cannot be easily translated or transferred to others.

Mission, not vision, is the first point at which most people connect

Figure 1. A Model for Nonprofit Management

with the idea behind an organization. An organization's mission explains what it is in business to do. With the mission in place and widely understood, nonprofits have the beginning of goal alignment in place. What's missing is some way to guide people on a daily basis, a way to bridge the gap between mission and action. That's the role of values. Which is a story for another day.

Once the mission is defined, understood, and agreed upon, the next step is to devise a strategy that will realize the mission. Strategy is a conceptual framework for aligning activities and decisions at all levels of the organization. Strategy answers the question: How will you achieve your mission? Strategy can be a bit more complicated to explain than the mission, though it shouldn't be too much more complicated or else it turns into a meaningless idea.

The strategy an organization implements should directly influence the way that the organization is structured. One strategy for accomplishing the mission may require one set of reporting structures and organizational divisions. Another strategy may require a completely different setup. The chosen strategy leads the nonprofit to make choices that fit on an organizational chart and in job descriptions. Once the structure is set, choices about how to allocate resources—people, money, equipment, etc.—get easier to make, or at least more logical. Finally, the realities of resource availability and use have a feedback effect on the mission, and the cycle starts all over again.

And now for some secrets. . .

PART ONE

Vision

VISION ▶ Dreams and Actions

Resources

Organizational Structure

Mission

Strategy

Dreams and Actions

Ever heard of an agency that is said to have lost its vision? Probably not often. But have you ever heard of an agency that is said to have lost its sense of mission? We hear that one just about every day. An unfocused sense of mission causes everything from financial troubles to organizational inertia. So why do we hear more about mission than vision? The answer has to do with the difference between vision and mission. We find that the two are often confused. Yet there is a great deal of difference between them.

Quoting dictionary definitions is ordinarily a sign of weak writing, but we'll bend that rule a bit and review some of the words and phrases that our reference sources used to describe these two concepts.

Vision	Mission
• Imagination	• A body of persons
• Dreams	• Office
• Forecasting	• Organization
• Mental picture	• Series of services

Look at these two lists of words. The words describing vision are words that also describe characteristics of individuals. The words describing mission, however, are words that also describe characteristics of organizations. Here is another way to say it: People have visions, organizations have missions.

THE ELEMENTS OF A VISION

True vision is a uniquely personal commodity. It is the dream that provides the impetus for all operations of an organization. Often, vision exists in the mind and heart of an organization's founder, and can be such a grandiose goal that it seems close to preposterous. The original vision of Millard Fuller, the founder of Habitat for Humanity, was a variation on the theme of economic equality, and other executives hold equally lofty visions. Their strength comes from the fact that if you stretch far enough, you're bound to accomplish many good things even if you fall short of your goal. As a colleague from Sri Lanka puts it, "to hit the top of the mango tree, shoot for the moon."

A leader's vision is outwardly focused. Few vision-holders think in terms of departments, governance structures, policies, and other details of administration. Rather, their starting point is the outside world and the organization's place in it. Operational details come later, usually from some other source. A vision is also firmly oriented toward the future with such a long-range quality to it that it can be hard to calculate in years the amount of time required to implement it.

Vision is important not for the details it provides but for the passion and urgency it supplies the visionary. Without the grandiose notions embodied in most visions, few would be inspired to take action. One implication of this is that a nonprofit can actually survive without a particularly strong vision. Usually it turns out to have been present sometime in the past—such as in the mind of the founder—and successors have simply remained faithful to its general outlines. Finally, vision is most important at the beginning of an organization's development, and at key junctures thereafter. Often when an organization hesitates to act at a critical juncture it's because no one provides the vision necessary to make sense of an otherwise seemingly risky path.

OTHER VISIONS COMPLEMENT

We've talked so far about a sole individual's vision, probably the executive director, as though no one else in the organization is eligible to act from a strong personal commitment. Since managers get caught up in day-to-day realities it can be hard for them to develop a coherent vision to carry them through all the ambiguities, which is one of the reasons for creating a widely accepted mission statement.

Still, people at all levels of the nonprofit can develop their own personal vision. The reason that these typically won't clash with the CEO/executive director's vision is that they are inevitably rooted in a particular position or function. In practice, such a manager's vision should act to support the overall vision. For example, the financial manager who operates from a personal vision of the future—as opposed to just putting out daily fires—ideally will complement the overall vision, even if it is never explicitly stated.

MISSION IS THE SOURCE OF MOTIVATION

As such a personal commodity, vision may or may not be present at any given time in an organization. Rather, the concepts embodied in the vision are captured in the mission which is an ever-present, clear articulation of organizational goals and purpose. In a for-profit company, employees understand that the primary mission is to be profitable. Shrewd managers take this a step further and develop other goals that are a bit more uplifting, but profitability has to be number one.

Because nonprofits do not have the same primary, and well-understood, goal of making a profit, they don't have this common driver around which to focus organizational energy. The structural motive to encourage cooperation and teamwork is lacking. Consequently, nonprofit leaders have to work especially hard to replace this natural unifier and motivator. A clear and engaging mission, drawn from a vision, helps to provide this unification and motivation. This is because a mission statement—and the strategy that grows out of it—helps the people of a nonprofit align their own goals and actions with the organization's strategic direction. In the nonprofit framework, the meaningful profit goes to the community.

PART TWO

Mission

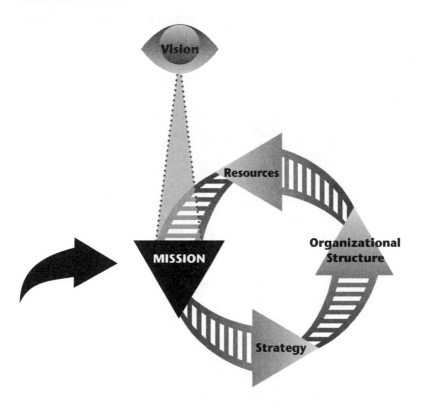

The Art of the Mission Statement, or Why the Writing *Should* Be on the Wall

Try this test.

Pull together a mixed group of staff members. Include people in program positions, managers, administrative staff, and any long-term consultants. Include that part-time staff member hired last month, as well as the administrative assistant who's been there longer than anyone else.

Now ask them all to take a piece of paper and write out the agency's mission. Ask them to pass the papers to the center of the table, unsigned. Compare the actual mission statement with some or all of the versions. You have just determined whether the organization has a workable mission statement.

The greater the degree of agreement between the actual mission statement and those submitted by the staff, the stronger the organization. The greater the differences, the less cohesive the organization is likely to be and, in the long run, the less effective it will be in achieving *any* mission.

Do the same exercise with board members, or any other group of stakeholders in a nonprofit organization. On the other hand, you might want to do this exercise only in your mind at first. The responses you receive may be quite revealing.

Everyone knows that a nonprofit organization must have a meaningful mission statement but achieving it is a lot harder than it sounds.

If there is too great a disparity among the individual responses the agency essentially does not even have a mission. Rather, it has a series of independent agendas that may or may not work well together.

THE ROLE OF THE MISSION STATEMENT

A mission statement is one of the few widely understood and visible tools for bringing people together. Most aspects of business life drive people apart. The competitiveness of all types of funding, individualized professional degrees, and most laws have the effect of splitting and compartmentalizing people and organizations.

A car rounding a curve stays on the road only if the gravitational forces pulling it off the road are exactly balanced by the gravitational forces pulling it back. Organizations stop working well when they can't find ways to counteract the forces pulling them off the road. A carefully crafted mission statement gives people—including the part-timer who just started last month—an invaluable means of keeping everyone on the road.

Shorter Is Sweeter

In order to perform its function, a mission statement should have a few key characteristics. First, it should be succinct. Take a cue from advertisers—punchy always beats ponderous. In a real sense, the mission statement is a small piece of advertising. Like a logo it should be distinct and communicate something important about the organization.

Relatively few organizations devise their own logo, even if it means they just find a graphic artist who's a friend of a friend and is willing to work cheap or free. Yet most organizations craft their own mission statements. This is probably because the mission statement is usually arrived at in the context of a group meeting, and the tendency to group-write seems natural.

However, a mission statement is really a narrative expression of enormous dreams and energy. The flattening, almost bureaucratic nature of most committee writing doesn't readily communicate richness. Although it may be overkill to solicit a professional writer to write a simple mission statement, a decent wordsmith who has sat through the planning meetings and has been exposed to the flavor of the group should be able to come up with a reasonable version.

In any case, the mission statement needs to be short because people need to remember it. The human mind is simply not capable of grasping more than a handful of variables at once. This is why when you order tuna salad on wheat you will get it without much trouble. But try ordering ham on rye with Swiss cheese, tomatoes, onions, sprouts, roasted red peppers, and spicy mustard on the side. Eventually, you'll probably get the sandwich prepared correctly— but the sandwich preparer is almost guaranteed to ask you to repeat your order at least once. A lot of mission statements are like complicated deli orders.

The other reason to craft a succinct mission statement is to provide a clear sense of organizational direction. A broad mission statement that leaves open every single eventuality may seem like a safe way to prepare for the future, but all it does is confuse people. It does not suggest a clear purpose for being. Ultimately a mission statement is about making choices, and if it does not clearly indicate a single reasonably flexible direction it invites confusion and practically assures wasted efforts.

What It Should *Not* Include

Statement of Markets
There is an understandable tendency to talk about markets in the mission statement—"we will provide our services to federal, state, and local governments interested in preventing homelessness." Leave the statement of markets for your business plan unless it is a particularly important part of your organization (such as a trade association that must respond to its members). Who you're planning to serve is a detail of business that isn't all that interesting to other people and may actually puzzle a few. If I represent a managed care organization interested in preventing homelessness among my members and I read the above mission, I would conclude that the agency isn't interested in working with us.

Statement of Quality
Our personal candidate for the least necessary item to include in the mission statement is a reference to providing quality services. *Of*

course you plan to provide quality services. Does anyone intend to provide poor services? This is just like the for-profit organization stating that it intends to be profitable: Is anyone truly motivated by that sentiment? Is it unique enough that it belongs up-front in the mission?

Frame It!

Once the mission statement is complete and acceptable, buy picture frames. The reason most people are unclear about their own organization's mission statement is that it isn't publicized. It doesn't take a massive advertising campaign to promote it. Depending on the physical layout of your organizational site(s), a few tastefully framed copies of the mission statement in the lobby, hallway, or waiting area make an impact. A copy also should be prominently displayed in the executive director's office.

Here are some other ideas for cheap but effective promotion of the mission statement. Some may not work if the statement is too long, but they might inspire alternatives.

- At the bottom of official letterhead
- As a framed and personalized copy for every new board member
- As screen savers in public places
- On the cover of the human resource policy manual
- Incorporated in consultants' contracts
- In every set of minutes from board meetings
- In every proposal for funding
- On preprinted directions sent to visitors
- As part of the postmark
- In the office-wide voicemail greeting
- On agency checks
- On invoices submitted for payment

Now get that mixed group of staff together and ask them to write down the mission statement. Do the job of promoting the mission statement properly, and many of them won't even need to look at the framed copy on the wall.

The Life Cycles of Nonprofit Organizations

L ike flowers, different types of nonprofits have predictable life cycles. At any one time, different types are at different points in those life cycles. Some struggle to survive, while others have settled into a comfortable corner. The services of some classes of nonprofits are practically household names while others must work hard just to get society to recognize what they do. The national population of nonprofits includes groups at every stage of development, like a flower garden.

We are not talking about individual nonprofits and their life cycles here, but rather recognizable categories of nonprofits. Why is the nonprofit life cycle important? Because where a category of nonprofit organizations finds itself on the life cycle continuum says a great deal about the likely success or failure of an individual manager. To put it another way, the forces characteristic of any one point on the continuum are so much stronger than the average manager that it takes a highly unusual person—or a great deal of luck—to buck the prevailing trends.

What follows is an attempt to suggest a framework for analyzing entire groups of nonprofits (as well as individual organizations). Use it to help in strategic positioning or to hire a new executive director. Most importantly, use it to get beyond the particulars of your situation and begin seeing your strategic direction as the product of systemic forces more potent than managers' skill sets or personalities alone.

THE SIX STAGES

In this model, there are six distinct stages in the development of non-profit service populations: forming, growing, coalescing, peaking, maturing, and refocusing. At each stage the developmental task for the category is different, and the definition of accomplishment varies. We will take each stage in turn.

Forming

In the forming stage a handful of similar organizations are just beginning to appear. Often, nonprofit organizations are created to deal with some type of dysfunction in another part of society. For instance, orphanages were created in part because the newly industrialized economy, unlike farm-based production, required parents to physically separate from their children for the workday. Further, unsafe working conditions sometimes killed or maimed the parents, making the separation permanent and creating the need to care for the now orphaned children.

The key here is that social and economic conditions affect large numbers of people all across the country the same way. Not surprisingly, local responses tend to resemble each other. In the 1980s, as the AIDS epidemic hit this country, organizations in different cities were created along similar lines, each one groping for constructive responses to the crisis. Today, a whole category of social enterprises has begun to assemble itself as existing nonprofits spin off entities to explore more entrepreneurial ways of providing services. And many of the nonprofit groups created to take advantage of the Internet could be considered a new category of organizations.

Growing

As the nonprofit members of a particular category refine their identity and collective vision, society responds with increased opportunities for growth. Innovative urban youth programs such as City Year are good examples of groups in the growth stage. Growth takes energy, so the primary characteristic of groups in this stage is that a great deal of resources and time are devoted to internal demands.

Coalescing

At some point the group of nonprofits begins to be recognized and accepted by society and by their peers. Some organizations step up to take a leadership role, while others spring up to fill the gaps left by the earlier entrants. This is the point at which most groups are aware of each other, having begun to form formalized local and national associations and other support entities. There is the beginning of a recognizable national identity—if a television show mentions the service type there's a good chance that most people will have at least a vague idea of what it is. Battered women's shelters seemed to have entered this stage in the 1990s.

Peaking

As a group, these nonprofits enjoy widespread recognition and unprecedented acceptance. Few new entrants spring up—consider the number of universities founded in the past 20 years—but the established organizations achieve steady victories. When consolidations occur they usually end up making an existing organization stronger. Health maintenance organizations in the 1990s moved from coalescing to peaking.

Maturing

Maturing nonprofits long ago hit their peak and are losing some of their strategic momentum. Often the services they provide are now being offered by others or in another way, or are no longer as necessary as they once were. At the same time, they have a kind of schizoid existence, since they are widely recognized community institutions. Their fundraising programs are firmly in place, their leaders have strong ties to the area, and their sheer longevity has created a pool of former employees and volunteers favorably disposed to the organization. No one can doubt their collective influence, but some are beginning to doubt their future. Hospitals are at this stage of development, as are federated fundraising organizations.

Refocusing

Once past maturity, some classes of nonprofits begin a slow drift. No longer the influential organizations of their peak and mature years, they nonetheless retain enough of a presence to ensure their continued survival—at least in the absence of some major external threat. Those that survive to begin the cycle all over again use this period to reinvent themselves. Many orphanages refocused themselves as special needs providers when various societal forces effectively ended their original missions. The American Lung Association refocused itself and changed its name when its original mission, the eradication of tuberculosis, was largely accomplished. This can be a long and painful process, however, and in the future we can expect more categories of nonprofits to enter this stage in greater numbers, particularly those that were founded during the 1960s and 1970s. For them, the question will be whether they can succeed in refocusing, and how quickly they can do it.

It is important not to reason backward from this model and conclude that every individual nonprofit organization goes through each of these stages. Individual agencies can leapfrog stages in any direction as a result of unique circumstances, but the majority of members of an identifiable class will follow these stages fairly faithfully. In some cases, whole categories of agencies may remain in a single group for a very long time. Also, many organizations have intuitively incorporated the ability to reinvent themselves, thereby carrying on a long-term refocusing effort even while they are at the peak of their development. In some ways, this is what successful colleges and universities are able to do all the time.

Still, streetsmart nonprofit managers will be able to use this framework to interpret and even predict the future for their own organizations. Each stage has different tasks that must be carried out and typically demands different types of people on the board and in management to accomplish them. Flowers aren't the only things that have seasons.

The Death (and Rebirth) of Advocacy

Advocacy organizations have a large and intimidating enemy. It's not governmental officials or an uneducated public. It's not public apathy or other well-endowed advocacy groups. The greatest enemy of advocacy organizations is success. Knowing how to influence public policy and resource allocation is hard enough, but knowing when to recognize success and how to shift methods when you achieve success is far more difficult.

This is partly why organized labor has lost so much influence in recent decades. The federal government has studied organized labor's agenda and responded with—*agreement*. Government officials have instituted programs and laws such as workers' compensation, unemployment insurance, and OSHA, which, bit by bit, bring into the government those functions which labor unions formerly advocated or might have carried out themselves. The irony is that employees are better off while unions suffer declining membership.

The rest of the nonprofit field is filled with similar examples. A large number of nonprofits began their institutional lives advocating for services for people with mental retardation and developmental disabilities. Others pushed for equal educational opportunities for special needs students. Many advocacy groups then turned to providing those services themselves, if only because no other groups had the same level of commitment and understanding.

FROM CLASS ADVOCACY TO INDIVIDUAL, FROM FEDERAL TO LOCAL

Meanwhile, a subtle shift occurred that challenges advocacy organizations to change their focus. Initially, advocacy meant educating the public about the nature of a problem, explaining its prevalence and what could be done about it. This was work done on behalf of an entire class of individuals. Then, as government and other revenue sources responded, the nature of advocacy changed. No longer was it on behalf of whole classes of individuals but rather on behalf of individuals themselves. For example, the right of all people to a public school education has been established, even for those with special needs. But specific individuals and their families often need individual advocacy to obtain full and proper services.

The second part of the challenge facing advocates is that information is easier to obtain. Computers and the Internet can actually do a more efficient job of spreading certain kinds of information than individual agencies are capable of doing. In some cases, employers are finding it advantageous to supply information as well.

Devolution on the federal level is affecting national advocacy organizations as responsibilities formerly centralized in Washington are handed over to the states. This is forcing national groups to work harder to hang on to advances, and it may create fifty smaller battlefields for new advocacy where only one was necessary before.

Finally, in many fields the revolution is over and it's time to start managing. The demands of success in nonprofit management have so intensified in recent years that whatever appetite may have existed for "pure" advocacy has given way to the pressing realities of running complex organizations.

THE CHANGING WORK OF ADVOCATES

The result is that what we understand as advocacy is changing. Here are a few of the ways that advocates will see the changes in their own work:

More advocacy will be done by managers. The tables have turned. Whereas in the past management was a logical outgrowth of successful advocacy, advocacy in the future will be part of successful management. Again, this is consistent with advocacy becoming more oriented to specific individuals rather than whole classes of individuals.

Just as advocates struggled to be managers, and in some cases decided they didn't want to be managers at all, managers in the future will need to assume some responsibility for advocacy. It will not always be a graceful match. Whenever the demands of the two roles conflict, management will usually predominate. Part of the solution will be to instill a tradition of advocacy in the hearts and minds of managers.

The biggest demand for advocacy will be from individuals. Once entitlements or broad programs are established, the major thrust for advocacy is from individuals demanding admission or a different share. Information and referral is a key service, which is why employers are emerging as major sources of assistance in areas such as dependent care and employee assistance. For example, in health care a new class of fee-for-service advocates hired to negotiate with HMOs on behalf of members may emerge shortly.

Most class-based advocacy will be successful through the legal system, not via traditional political routes. Legislatures around the country are showing little desire to add more entitlements unless they are forced to do so through the legal system. Shrewd advocates have already made this shift. An interesting aspect of this change is that legal advocacy is relatively more productive; a single lawsuit can bring about greater change than dozens of lobbying campaigns.

The work of advocates will change. The sum of all this is that the day-to-day work of many advocates will change. With the exception of groups responding to unforeseen societal demands such as the AIDS epidemic, advocacy interests must adapt to the new realities of individualized, local advocacy. The line between advocates and managers will be much less clear, and the advocacy of interests will need to be built into the larger systems that deliver the services. Ombudsmen are a good example of institutional provisions that will flower in the new systems.

Good advocates will always feel like their work is never done, and they are right. But the nature of that work and the way it gets carried out are changing just as the targets of advocacy are changing. To stay effective, advocacy must change as well.

The End of a Mission

What's wrong with this picture? It's the annual meeting of a very visible and well-regarded corporation. With the pleasantries over and the introductions complete, the president takes the podium. "Good afternoon, ladies and gentlemen," the president begins. "You all know what a wonderful organization we have here. It began with a small meeting in my living room, and today we have a presence in virtually every state in the union. Our accomplishments are recognized as far away as Australia and Brazil. National political leaders constantly seek our advice, and hardly a month goes by without someone from our organization being quoted in the *Wall Street Journal*.

"We have much of which we can all be proud. We are in good financial shape, and our leadership remains dedicated and energetic. We have accomplished exactly what we set out to do. Therefore, effective tomorrow, we are closing down. Thank you, and goodbye."

What corporation—nonprofit or for-profit—chooses to close its doors at the height of its power? What type of people can walk away from salaries, fringe benefits, organizational prestige, and institutional power? One organization that did just that was Action for Children's Television (ACT), the Cambridge, Massachusetts-based gadfly for quality commercial children's television.

When ACT founder and executive director Peggy Charren announced that the 24-year-old agency would be closing its doors, it was only one of a long string of unconventional choices. What this former children's book fair organizer and one-time aspiring librarian accomplished was nothing short of the reformulation of part of an entire industry. In the process she and her staff showed us how

24

our information-age society can change itself, and how carefully designed and well-managed nonprofit organizations can drive that process of change.

A major element of ACT's success is that its timing was, in Charren's words, "excruciatingly wonderful." She and her suburban friends started the agency in 1968 at a time when the first generation of children exposed to commercial television from infancy was coming of age, and well before current social problems were even vaguely articulated. "Today . . ." said Charren, "if I tried to start this kind of thing I'd be laughed at." Another ingredient in ACT's success was its relatively narrow focus of forcing governmental agencies to ensure that children have ample choices in television programming and campaigning against deceptive child-related advertising.

The Reagan years temporarily sidetracked ACT by emaciating much of the governmental muscle their original strategy had counted on, so they turned their attention to Congress instead. The agency's trips to Washington and Charren's never-ending media cultivation finally paid off when Congress passed the Children's Television Act of 1990. The Act specified that service to children is part of broadcasters' historical requirement to serve the public interest and that this particular audience requires specific attention.

The whole point of ACT was not to censor existing programming but to create a market and some political leverage for quality children's television programming. Closing its doors was a purely strategic decision, a signal that the battle for quality programming had to broaden its base and be fought in each media market rather than nationally by a single organization.

ACT gave us a peek at the nonprofit organization of the future. Nonprofit organizations reflect the times that created them. Our mass-production world in the earlier part of this century gave us massive hospitals, schools, and museums. Today the truly important space for most business organizations is measured in megabytes, and nonprofit organizations have to be constructed similarly. Whether the mission is to provide meals to AIDS patients in their homes, leverage investments in low-income housing, or promote innovation in software, today's new nonprofit organizations are likely to be highly focused entities designed to fill clear strategic roles.

ACT tells us that serving the public good in the next century, as nonprofit public charities are intended to do, may mean learning how to close up shop. ACT had to work hard to get its friends to understand that it was really closing. At one point its "Dear Friend" form letter explaining the closing featured a handwritten P.S. from Peggy Charren reading "I hope it is obvious that this means you should *not* send any more money to ACT!"

During the course of its existence, ACT taught us many valuable things. Its closing taught us another: that many nonprofit organizations know how to rise to the occasion, but only the very best have the vision to know when it's time to sit down.

PART THREE

Strategy

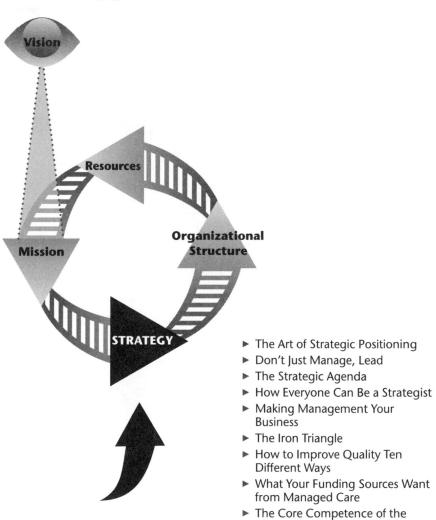

- ▶ The Art of Strategic Positioning
- ▶ Don't Just Manage, Lead
- ▶ The Strategic Agenda
- ▶ How Everyone Can Be a Strategist
- ▶ Making Management Your Business
- ▶ The Iron Triangle
- ▶ How to Improve Quality Ten Different Ways
- ▶ What Your Funding Sources Want from Managed Care
- ▶ The Core Competence of the Nonprofit Corporation
- ▶ A Different Kind of Growth
- ▶ Collaborating to Compete
- ▶ The Power of Social Enterprise
- ▶ Needed: Clearly Marked Exits

The Art of
Strategic Positioning

One thing that those involved with the nonprofit sector regard as an emerging fact is that strategic planning for nonprofit organizations is here to stay. It's time for a reconsideration. A peculiar and rarely recognized thing about nonprofit organizations is that they are, individually and institutionally, one of the most conservative sectors of our society. There are myriad reasons for this situation, ranging from legal and economic to cultural and social, but the end result is that they are generally slow to change.

One effect of this characteristic is that nonprofit organizations act as a kind of social buffer, mediating and differentiating the process of change throughout their own organizations and those they serve. Another effect is that the organizations that do understand how to change are able to read the signals properly and get out in front of the broad changes. Over time, this capacity makes them dominant in their fields. This is why certain hospitals, for example, were able to grow so effectively and fully during the 1950s and 1960s when federally influenced expansion capital was readily available and the seeds of today's technology-intensive health care were being sown.

In the past several years, as the economy soured and the demands on nonprofits soared, many nonprofit organizations turned to the kind of strategic planning that blue chip and Fortune 500 companies had busied themselves with in the 1970s and 1980s. The results, while somewhat encouraging in the short term, have been mixed over time. There are two major reasons for this state of affairs. First, as institutional buffers to change, many existing nonprofit organizations are profoundly reactive in their missions and, therefore, cannot or do not want to bear the same relationship with their environment as for-profit businesses might. Hospitals deal with people already sick, nursing homes with the frail, social service agencies with the previously abused or neglected, etc.

The second is that strategic planning doesn't work anyway. Especially for nonprofits. What does work is a much different approach. When the history of American business in the latter half of the twentieth century is written, it will be noted with some bemusement that great numbers of executives were arrogant enough to believe that they could actually plan the future of their organizations. It will be noted that millions of notebooks and megabytes were filled with careful research about every conceivable aspect of strengths, weaknesses, opportunities, and threats, and that skillfully produced and voluminous plans were printed with sincerity and gusto.

It will also be noted that the very best nonprofit organizations of the times already knew how to do it better. What the successful nonprofit organization knows how to do—often without consciously stating it as such—is strategic positioning rather than strategic planning. The adaptable nonprofit's ability to position itself grows out of its commitment to a mission. In exactly the same way that Apple Computer Company was a by-product of Steve Jobs' and Steve Wozniak's desire to democratize the computer world, the enduring nonprofit organization has a commitment to mission that transcends the particulars of its shape at any one moment.

When a nonprofit organization arrives at a statement of its strategic position formally and collectively, it creates a powerful gyroscope for leadership and decision-making. Further, it is a vision that can be widely acted upon as well. Traditional strategic planning works best in a traditional command and control type of organization. It doesn't work as well in a nonprofit setting for two reasons. First, in the absence of a universally agreed upon standard of success or failure, command and control in the military sense of the term is impossible.

Second, most nonprofit organizations do not have a traditional hierarchical structure as much as they have a series of interconnecting networks (even hospitals, which can seem intensely hierarchical, are actually composed largely of networks based on class and social standing). Strategic positioning comes more easily for nonprofit organizations because they tend to be so firmly grounded in their mission. To the extent that everyone understands and accepts that mission, devising a strategic position to fulfill it becomes an exercise in synthesis and consensus that produces far more widespread and genuine commitment than top down command and control could possibly produce. This is the reason that many nonprofits are actually more strategically sophisticated than their for-profit counterparts.

The final reason for the superiority of strategic positioning over strategic planning for nonprofit organizations is mundane but important; a good statement of strategic position is simply easier to communicate. It can be circulated to all levels without the inherent complexities and subsequent adjustments that a formalized plan usually entails, and it goes out of date much slower. Nonprofit organizations do not usually start out with advantages over other types of entities, but in the area of strategic leadership the thoughtful agency can capitalize on a few.

Rather than traditional strategic planning, whose product is a report that is often quickly abandoned and rendered out-of-date, *strategic positioning* creates a more enduring product. Strategic positioning answers the questions "What does the organization want to *be?* What is the perception in the environment that the organization seeks?" It is the role an organization seeks to establish in comparison to other players and factors in its operating environment.

Good strategies must be quickly understood in order to motivate and guide people. Strategy, to be effective, needs to be easy to transmit from person to person. As a result, it has to be relatively simple and free of distractions. A strategic position for a research organization might be to become everyone's first choice as co-principal investigator in its field on all federal grants of less than a million dollars. For a mental retardation/developmental disabilities service provider agency, it might be to be the "front door" to services for all infants and toddlers in its county. A home care agency may seek to be the market leader in home health services in its area. Whatever the choice, a strategic position defines the way in which an organization organizes itself to achieve its mission.

Planning strategy is different than planning work, though the two are inherently connected. Strategy is the force that guides the work and gives it a sense of direction and purpose. Both strategy and work are important to a well-run organization, but our focus for now is on the strategy side.

Strategy isn't the mission either. Strategy is that set of broad behaviors and objectives put in place in order to accomplish the mission. Both should be easily expressed, but the mission statement
should take the high road. Strategy is the first stop in management
country.

DO BE DO BE DO

Recently we were speaking to one of those elder statesmen of the
nonprofit world who devote a substantial chunk of their retirement
to serving on nonprofit boards. His boards were all workhorse
organizations—no fancy, big-name organizations for this hard-
working volunteer. Yet he had a lament about all four of them. "All
of my nonprofit agencies are going through strategic planning processes," he said. "And every single one of those plans is going to fail."

Undoubtedly he was right. Strategic thinking often isn't done correctly. The result is muddled leadership, missed opportunities, and
a generalized distrust of strategic planning. This is unfortunate,
since nonprofits need to be strategically shrewder than ever before.

To evaluate your agency's strategic plan, read through it quickly
to get a flavor for the details. If the document is about what you're
going to *be*, it's a strategic plan. If it contains a lot of detail about what
you're going to *do*, it's a work plan.

The difference is critical, and it derives from a simple difference
between strategy and management. To put it simply, strategy deals
with matters of leadership and change. By contrast, management
planning and implementation deals with complexity.

Because good strategies are simple and almost visceral, they are
more likely to unite people. In this respect, they are like mission
statements, a kind of internal public declaration. Strategy must flow
from a common understanding of the external environment and be
consistent with the values of the organization. These are all things
that are forward-looking and tend to be pivotal matters in crucial activities like hiring. Employees either accept these things or choose to
work elsewhere. This self-selects for people who will provide a base
of agreement with the strategy.

Strategy should be the prime focus of the board of directors and
senior managers. Simple statements of strategy are more readily understood by board members who do not have intimate knowledge

of the agency's field. Strategic objectives can be used to support other activities such as evaluating the executive director. Board members don't need to have particularly specialized knowledge to carry out this crucial task when they have the benefit of a good strategy.

By contrast, work plans are products of the intellect. They require concentration to absorb and possibly even detailed knowledge to truly understand. More important, they tend to divide people. If managers see an element of a work plan that threatens to reduce their budget or influence, they will naturally oppose it—even if they agree with the overall strategy.

What often passes for strategic planning is really work planning. Detailed, cross-referenced lists of goals, objectives, responsible persons, and deadlines are excellent tools for the day-to-day manager. But if they are elevated to the level of strategies, the organization is almost certain to miss the unifying effect that true strategy can bring.

All of which is not to say that strategy is superior to implementation planning. Both are necessary, and each contributes something different to an organization. So the ideal is to devise a process in which each can flourish.

Start with strategy. The organization's strategy should flow naturally from its mission. It should be able to be stated succinctly, preferably as a strategic position. It will take time to develop, which is why it usually requires an off-site retreat or at least a series of thoughtful meetings dedicated to the task. Strategy is a symphony, not an accordion player. A talented CEO might be able to develop a perfectly respectable strategy, but it is unlikely to be embraced by the full organization as quickly or efficiently as a collaboratively developed strategy would be. Even if the eventual strategy seems obvious to some, the act of devising it strengthens the organization in a way that won't happen otherwise.

The strategic position should be achievable through a small number of very specific objectives. Similar to the strategy, these objectives should be general and long-term in nature. Consider them goals, not tasks. For example, an essential objective of the "front door" strategy would be to develop the ability to maintain large amounts of data, of varying kinds, spanning several years. The home health leader strategy, like all market leader strategies, would necessitate a sophisticated promotional and public relations capability, volume-based pricing, research capability, and strong quality systems.

Stop right there. That's it for strategy, because the next step is up to management. *This* is when that multi-page document with copious detail gets produced (be careful, because it's all that careful detail that causes the thing to be ignored, no matter who produces it). It should dovetail exactly with the strategic position, taking the handful of objectives and putting implementation details into them.

Of the two documents—and there should be two distinctly different documents—it's the statement of strategy that should be the longest-lived. The management plan will probably have to change as soon as the first draft is printed, but that's okay. It's a management tool with a much shorter time horizon than the strategy. If the latter is any good, it should last at least two or three years before needing significant revisions, and perhaps even longer.

THE FIVE ELEMENTS OF A STRATEGIC POSITION

A strategic position should speak to five specific elements:

- demand for service
- services provided by the organization
- geography covered by the agency
- the competition
- the resources used (money, people, etc.)

By defining these five elements, an organization will help determine much of its strategic position. To work with others to develop a strategy, try walking through the five elements that comprise a good strategic position.

The Demand for Service

Nonprofits exist to fill a need. Often, that need exists because of some sort of personal dysfunction or structural gap in society. Shelters for abused women, mental health clinics, and special needs education programs all exist for some combination of these two reasons.

The first part of strategy analysis involves knowing who demands the service that you provide. For health and human service programs it's a matter of knowing who feels the pain, for think tanks it's who needs the information, for cultural groups it's who desires the experience, and so on.

The frequent presence of third party payors, such as health insurance, foundation grants, and public school systems' outsourcing programs, means it is often difficult to determine the true client, or user of a service. When the user is not the payor it creates some rich paradoxes and riddles. Personally, we have had many fascinating philosophical conversations about who is the *true* client in nonprofit services, but the demands of running an agency preclude open-ended ruminations about philosophies. One simply has to decide who has the greatest decision-making power in one's own setting and go on from there.

When a nonprofit gets paid from a substantial number of third-party arrangements, a useful way to think about the demand for service is to consciously separate who pays for the service from who demands that it be delivered. The answer will vary. For example, the teenager in trouble with the law may be the client of a youth services program, but it's society in general via the court system that demands service on behalf of him or her. What the teenager thinks and wants is relatively less important than what the judges want. On the other hand, in traditional fee-for-service Medicaid programs, individual clients have the power while Medicaid acts largely as a behind-the-scenes payor (Medicaid managed care systems dramatically change the equation by stepping directly into the classic transaction).

Determining who demands the service and has the power to influence the choice is no easy matter. This is why market research is always an essential component of delivering a service. Most nonprofits don't do market research because they don't have to—a government entity or some other participant has already established the need. The incidence of cancer or learning disabilities is fairly consistent, for example, so it is often possible to infer a great deal about one's own area on the strength of others' research. The basic strategy question is whether the underlying details of the demand may have changed, such as when demographics shift or disease prevention activities begin to succeed.

Services Provided

Every nonprofit crafts its own response to demands for services. These are typically called programs or services. Sometimes the service is clearly defined. A Mahler symphony is the same for everyone who plays it, so the value of performing it lies in the interpretation. But most of those who demand services—and many of the entities that pay for it—haven't thought systematically about what they want. Twenty-four hours in a nursing home is the same time period for everyone, but for some it involves extensive life support technology while for others it is little more than assurance of health and safety. In between is a lot of gray area.

Programs and services are the area of greatest variation for most nonprofits, both in execution and in quality. Without widespread agreement about what constitutes quality in most health and human services, payors and their providers have had to make up the models as they go along. In the absence of Mahler symphonies, the key is to understand the needs and resources of the demand and match the nature of the supply with the demand.

Geography

The third area of strategy is geographic coverage. No matter how large and sophisticated nonprofits may grow, they are still largely local organizations. For-profit companies may span the continent and even the world, but most nonprofits are inescapably local (or regional at most). The challenge is determining the definition of local in each case.

Many years ago in the health care field a variety of planning and funding efforts attempted to carefully define local service areas. In most cases these definitions are now defunct, though nonprofits may still act as though there are active boundaries. There is no intrinsic problem with that, as long as the boundaries are clear and as long as the nonprofit has no illusions about how protected from competition it is.

Ultimately, geography is really just the most common way of segmenting the demand for services. There are other ways too, such as populations served or administrative boundaries imposed by an outside agent such as a national "corporate" office. However these boundaries are determined, they will be explicit in the eventual strategy.

The Competition

Finally, an intelligent strategy must consider the competition. Others providing the same service will be going through more or less the same planning process, and their strategies will often have an impact on everyone else.

Some competition is easily identifiable. Most organizations' managers are at least somewhat aware of who provides similar services to similar populations in the same geographic area. But in a more and more competitive nonprofit world with less and less respect for geographic distance, it is entirely possible that competitors cannot be identified. We once worked with a research institute that competes both locally and nationally. With that kind of strategy it is virtually impossible to determine all of one's potential competitors. Their competition must be understood as an undifferentiated capability that thousands of organizations could possess.

Some nonprofits are evolving a more sophisticated view of competition in which they simultaneously compete and collaborate with each other. Many for-profits do this all the time, as when competing airlines have backroom systems that allow them to transfer tickets and payments to unsnarl travel problems. Mergers and alliances are another example of how nonprofits are redefining the rules of competition. These considerations should all be part of devising the strategy as it relates to competitors.

Resources

Underlying the previous four elements are the resources needed to knit them all together. Resources include the basics such as personnel, money, technology, and tangible assets. It also may include intangibles such as reputation and intellectual property, which may be every bit as critical to doing the job as more tangible items. This is the arena in which the organization backs up its convictions by assigning the things of value which it controls to accomplishing the strategy. Because it is also the site of many individual disputes, the pattern of distributing resources is the surest way to infer what activities and programs a nonprofit truly regards as important.

Strategy, of course, is more than the sum of a few elements, and a good statement of strategic position can touch on other factors as well. However, the demand for service, the services themselves, geography, competition, and resources constitute the irreducible five of a comprehensive strategy.

Our friend, the elder statesman, intuitively understood the problems with a lot of strategic plans. To avoid them, just remember the difference between planning work and planning strategy—between *do* and *be*. It's more than just a few bars of an old timer's song.

Don't Just Manage, Lead

One of the lasting truisms of this field is that non-profits should become more businesslike. It is said that nonprofit managers need to develop management skills. Agencies must be managed more professionally. People who succeed in programs and get promoted to management positions need management training.

This is all true. There are more than 700,000 nonprofit public charities in this country, up from 400,000 just 10 years ago. Every one of them needs at least one manager, and the majority need far more than that. The supply of skilled managers specifically trained in the nonprofit field cannot even approach the demand, and so for the foreseeable future we can expect a chronic shortfall. This is one of the reasons why colleges and universities around the country are rushing to initiate or expand nonprofit management programs.

But in our justifiable hurry to bring sound management principles and practices to nonprofit organizations, we tend to overlook a central irony: Even more than good managers, nonprofit agencies need good leaders. The reasons are firmly rooted in the interplay between a rapidly changing external environment and the unique internal management characteristics of nonprofit organizations.

THE WAY IT (PROBABLY) USED TO BE

One can easily imagine the implied contract, two or three generations ago, between a nonprofit board of directors and its executive director. It probably went something like this: "We're the trustees of this place, and so we're accountable for it. You manage. We'll lead."

This simple formula worked well for many years. The accountability part still does. On the whole, members of a nonprofit's board of directors tend to incorporate the larger community's expectations, and are mindful of their fiduciary responsibility. Acting responsibly is something that most boards know how to do.

But the leadership part has subtly changed. During the past two or so generations, the nonprofits themselves have evolved. First, there are many more of them. Moreover, they are much more complicated. Hospitals have become huge enterprises. Health and social service nonprofits are subject to byzantine funding policies. Regulatory requirements abound for most nonprofits, and organizations of all kinds are experimenting with new programming, new services, and new markets.

In order to work intelligently on a strategic level, one needs a basic understanding of the industry in which one operates. Unfortunately, today's board members rarely have the time to gain even part of the knowledge they need to be effective leaders in their agency's field. So they turn to the executive director and his or her team, if any, for much of that strategic vision.

As long as there is a true leader somewhere on the staff, the delegation of authority works all right. When everyone is managing and no one is leading, the agency can get into trouble. In the health and social service fields this is why the prospect of managed care causes so much anxiety. Were the details and exact outlines of managed care to be known, they could be managed. Since no one usually knows those details until they are actually implemented, the only possible response while waiting is leadership. If no one exercises that leadership, the organization drifts.

LEADERS VERSUS MANAGERS

What is the difference between managers and leaders? This is one of those topics that can be endlessly debated. The chart on the next page tries to summarize one way of looking at this question.

Look closely at the entries in both columns. If there is a single common theme, it has to do with time horizons. Managers' time horizons are necessarily short—this afternoon, tomorrow, next week, next month. In many cases they must deal with things that have already happened. Moreover, there is a kind of universal quality to good

Leaders	Managers
Cope with change	Cope with complexity
Anticipate crises	Resolve crises
Increase revenue	Cut spending
Invest	Spend
Focus on concepts	Focus on personalities
Shape and influence	Control and tinker

management. John Kotter, in *The Leadership Factor,* calls management "a set of explicit tools and techniques . . . designed to be used in remarkably similar ways across a wide range of business situations."

Leaders, on the other hand, need to carry out their responsibilities with a time frame measured in months and years. They also need to have a thorough grounding in their own industry. In this way, management truly is more of a generic activity than leadership.

Two points are important here. The differing orientations to time are neither good nor bad. Both are necessary in any organization of any size. They must be constantly balanced, and the nature of that balance will change over time.

The second point is that we're really talking about actions of the mind, not job descriptions. This means that it is neither possible nor desirable to neatly separate management from leadership. It also means that the same person can act as a manager at one time and as a leader at another time.

The major problem for many nonprofit managers seeking to be leaders is the internal environment in which they must operate. Small nonprofit organizations with limited resources tend to stifle attempts at true leadership. When the receptionist calls in sick and the copy machine breaks down in the middle of a big job it's hard to exercise leadership. Leadership in large organizations can be equally difficult for reasons ranging from bureaucratic inertia to staff infighting.

Happily, leadership can, to some extent, be learned. In the end, it is largely a state of mind. Yes, there are *natural* leaders, but in truth they are rare and most organizations are lucky to find even one. Instead, the rest of their managers must learn to do a little less managing and a little more leading.

The Strategic Agenda

Most strategic plans are dead as soon as the laser-jet prints the final copy. The reason? They never had a chance at implementation. Assuming that all of the covert and overt agendas have been appropriately considered in a plan's construction, the major reason why strategic plans fail to be implemented is because most organizations don't incorporate the strategic thrust of the plan into their daily operations.

There are several aspects of operations that should be based on the strategic plan, including internal and external communications, manager evaluations, and internal benchmarking. But, pound for pound, the single most important tool for implementing strategy direction is the agenda for board and staff meetings. Since management teams and their meetings tend to be widely different from agency to agency while board meetings tend to resemble each other more, we will concentrate on board meetings.

BORED MEETINGS

Here is one of the worst kept secrets of the nonprofit world: board meetings can be mind-numbingly boring.

Worse, they can be frustrating. Not frustrating in a table-thumping, vein-popping fashion, but frustrating in that participants often feel a muted sense of wasted opportunity without being able to identify the cause. Since most participants usually bring to the meetings the best of intentions and the noblest of aspirations, this frustration has an added cost in wasted energies.

The root of the problem can be found in the excerpt from a hypo-

I. Executive director's report
  A. Information technology plan update

II. Finance committee report
  A. Analysis of overall agency profitability
  B. Analysis of new program profitability
  C. Cash flow and investment needed for new program
  D. Consideration of next phase of technology capital investment
  E. Proposed change in insurance agency

III. Nominating committee update
  A. New candidates report

IV. Program committee report
  A. Documentation of need for new program

Figure 2. Typical Board of Directors' Agenda (Excerpt)

thetical nonprofit board meeting agenda in Figure 2. The repetitive backward-looking nature of the agenda, consisting entirely of reports and updates, is obvious. For a board member seeking to use his or her skills and knowledge to advance the cause, it is depressingly flat. The underlying message is that the board meeting is a passive exercise, consisting of one long, unbroken string of lectures. Worse, the homogeneity of the agenda obscures any signals about what is important and what is not. Even if it did somehow communicate importance, there is no indication how this meeting relates to any other meeting, or to the overall mission of the organization. No one has much fun with this type of agenda, and very little is likely to get accomplished.

MAKE THEM STRATEGIC

Now look at the strategic agenda displayed in Figure 3. This agenda is based on a strategic plan which lists three top objectives, in order of importance, for the coming year: Expand the agency's existing educational program into the East Side of town; begin a five year plan to create an information technology infrastructure; and increase profitability.

The thinking behind the agenda goes like this. Since program expansion is the top priority, and since this meeting occurs at the start

> I. Expand educational program into East Side
>   A. Documentation of need (Program)
>   B. Analysis of program profitability (Finance)
>   C. Cash flow and investment needed (Finance)
>   D. Potential board member from East Side (Nominating)
>
> II. Increase profitability
>   A. Analysis of overall agency profitability (Finance)
>   B. Proposed change in insurance agency (Finance)
>
> III. Development of information systems
>   A. Discussion of five-year information technology plan (Executive)
>   B. Consideration of next phase of capital investment (Finance)

Figure 3.   Strategic Board of Directors' Agenda (Crosswalked with Figure 2)

of the year, the program goal should be the top agenda item. The agenda says that board members will be reviewing, perhaps for the final time, a study of the need for the program (note that this and all other written material should have gone out to board members at least several days before the meeting, though not so early that they will postpone reading them until it's too late). Next in importance is to be sure that everyone understands the investment that will be needed. This would cover such things as investments in equipment or real estate, up-front money to support cash flow, and the hidden cost of staff time in starting up the program. Both of these points should be covered by the finance committee and should entail liberal amounts of time for discussion.

The final part of the agenda is a bit more long range. The nominating committee has identified potential board members with significant ties to the East Side who are keenly interested in helping the organization expand there. The program expansion objective has given the nominating committee's work a concrete focus, and in this meeting they will present the candidates along with their recommendations.

Next up, if we were going in strict order of priority, would be the information technology objective. However, the work for tonight's meeting in this area is judged by the board president and executive director to be less of a priority than that in the profitability area, so the objectives will be flip-flopped just for this time.

As requested, the finance committee prepared its long-awaited study of agency profitability and distributed it to board members several weeks ago. The committee envisions this process as a long one, and is mainly interested in educating the rest of the board members about its philosophy and its plan. However, one item in its study stood out so starkly that there was no reason to delay taking action on it. As a result of years of indifference and neglect, the organization was clearly paying far more than it needed to for virtually all of its insurance coverage. Some hard work has produced a new insurance agency willing to supply the same coverage for a 25 percent savings. The finance committee is seeking approval from the board for this switch, since it involves such a large part of operational expenses.

The information technology five-year plan is just beginning, which is why it became the third item on this meeting's agenda. The executive director has taken responsibility for this project, and will explain how it will unfold in the coming years (the written outline was part of the material for the meeting). Related minor capital improvements, researched and recommended for approval by the finance committee, comprise the third item.

This kind of strategic agenda planning has two advantages. First, it draws board members away from the inherently backward-looking nature of reports and updates and involves them in future-oriented discussion and debate. Most of the content of the second agenda could very well have occurred under the first agenda. The difference is that material in the first agenda is compartmentalized, while the second agenda makes it easier to see the linkage between the items and the overall purpose and to produce informed discussion.

The second advantage is that it creates a sense of momentum and teamwork toward a common goal. The goals board members worked so hard to identify during their strategic planning retreat appear exactly as crafted on every board meeting agenda. Members know that they will be able to engage in the dialog, and the back-and-forth nature of committee material makes it easier for them to engage in the discussion because there won't be long stretches of time when they will be expected to be passive listeners.

There are many other techniques to assist an agency to achieve its goals, but basing ordinary board meetings on established long-range objectives is one of the easiest and most effective. Planning strategically has achieved its rightful status as a desirable activity for nonprofit organizations of all kinds. Planning for strategic implementation should be next on the agenda.

How Everyone Can Be a Strategist

Many people in nonprofit organizations now recognize the classic strategic planning recipe. Create a committee of board members and staff, do some preliminary planning, hold an off-site retreat for a day or two, devise a written plan, and spend the next several years implementing and reworking it. This is a time-tested, proven framework for developing a reliable strategic agenda for any organization.

As someone who makes part of his living by facilitating such sessions, I find this to be a very useful model. However, it carries an insidious message that, if taken too seriously, could prevent a nonprofit from ever developing to its fullest extent. That message goes something like this: *Strategy is only done by carefully selected people at certain times.* It is as though strategy is created only under controlled, laboratory-like conditions. After that, it's back to the daily grind.

In reality, strategy gets formulated in many different ways in a multitude of circumstances. A board member's casual comment, a staff member's well thought-out memo, a quick hallway conversation prior to an important meeting—these are just a sample of the sources for strategies that the entire organization may later embrace. The trick is to create an environment in which strategic insights have the greatest possible chance to flourish regardless of where they originated.

One way to begin setting the stage for such events—let's call them occasions of planned serendipity—is to understand the nature of strategy. For our purposes, nonprofit strategy can be said to have

46

Figure 4. Three Types of Work Done in Most Nonprofit Organizations

two distinct characteristics: it must be conceptual, and it must be future-oriented.

Figure 4 shows the three general types of work done in most nonprofit organizations—program, supervisory, and conceptual.

The direct service (or technical) level represents the vast amount of work done in most nonprofits. These are the program services, the "backroom" support services, and everything else of a technical or instrumental nature. This work is typically focused on achieving some sort of specified outcome. It is what is done by teachers in a school, therapists in a clinic, accountants in the finance department, and the receptionist who supports them all. It is most of the things recognized as "activities" in a nonprofit.

The next type of work, usually much less in quantity, consists of supervisory positions. This kind of work is self-explanatory, and is more or less intense according to the nature of the services and the workforce being supervised. It is the infrastructure, the oversight, and the organizational skeleton of the agency.

The final kind of work is conceptual in nature. This is activity carried out in the realm of ideas and has no direct connection with either an immediate task nor the oversight of staff. It is about passion, clear thinking, understanding the future, and defining purpose. This is where organizational strategy must take root.

All three terms should be understood in the context of the organization, not a particular individual's activity. For example, even though a professor may teach a highly conceptual course, his or her activity is nonetheless part of the productiveness of the college and has nothing to do with its overall strategy.

Strategy is also, by necessity, future oriented, though in a broad way. The time frame is usually unspecified and measured in years. Other activities may involve the future too, but not so sweepingly. The manager who makes out the weekly staff schedule is dealing with the future, but over a much shorter term.

Starting with the premise that strategy is conceptually based and future-oriented, it is easy to see how just about anyone who desires to do so can make a contribution to a nonprofit's strategy. We'll take a few common examples.

FINANCIAL MANAGERS

Financial managers deal so often with transactions that have already occurred that it can permanently color their thinking. Yet forward-looking financial managers can have an extremely powerful voice in strategy simply by looking ahead in their area of expertise.

The starting point for financial strategy is organizational strategy. Financial managers have to align financial incentives and choices with the overall direction of the organization. Take a high-growth strategy, for instance. In a high-growth mode with no endowment, the financial manager must protect liquidity at all costs, since failing to keep up with the constantly increasing cash demand would quickly stunt growth. That means that the manager must find a way to ensure high profitability. The manager will probably need to borrow aggressively, which in turn means that he or she will need to spend an above average amount of time working with the agency's bankers. All of these demands spell out a fairly detailed financial management strategy.

PROGRAM PEOPLE

Program people—they might be called things like curators, medical directors, deans, or head teachers—need to know the trends in their markets. They have to know exactly who their customer is—not always easy in a nonprofit setting. Early intervention service directors need to know that the trend is away from center-based early intervention, and mental health directors have to understand that advances in psychopharmacology can dramatically change the way they will provide services in five years. Art directors and curators must be able to book exhibits years in advance based on current changes in public taste.

Nonmanagement program people usually represent a nonprofit organization's greatest source of untapped potential for strategic insights. There are normally a lot of them, they are closest to the "customers," and they are not distracted by management's concerns. The major reason why they rarely contribute to strategy formulation is because they are not asked. Two ways to fix this: ask them and include them. This means that planners need to find ways to directly and continuously ask nonmanagement types for strategic insights into ways that they can respond (in English, not management-speak). It also means setting aside one or more seats on the planning group for people who don't normally get to sit at the planning table.

HUMAN RESOURCE MANAGERS

Three quarters of the average nonprofit's budget goes toward personnel costs, which is just another way of saying that the quality of the people who work for the agency determine virtually everything about its services. But who are these people? And will the answer to that question change in the next five years as the demographics of the local labor force change? What type of worker should the agency be attempting to attract in the future, and how does that translate into the design of the benefits plan? Will the agency's overall strategy be helped by changing the prerequisites for key jobs? What is the trade-off between employment and the use of technology? Should recruitment be emphasized, or retention?

COMPUTER PEOPLE

Like financial people, computer people can have a major impact on strategy. Most of the time this occurs through one seemingly small and unconnected computer decision at a time. IBM or Mac? Database or spreadsheet? New accounting software or an e-mail system? Owing to the extremely technical nature of managing computers, the dialog rarely gets beyond this level and information strategy is therefore established indirectly. But a computer person who understands the needs of the program staff and the financial staff and who can translate those things into concrete steps will have as large an impact on a nonprofit's strategic health as any one individual is likely to enjoy.

DEVELOPMENT STAFF

Finally, development staff represent the way that a good measure of strategy gets funded. By coordinating development choices with program and financial strategies, they can support key areas of the organization.

Strategic contributions can come from anyone in a nonprofit organization if they understand how to think about their job in conceptual and future-oriented ways. That doesn't mean that the ideas will be used, of course, but that is a different matter for a different time. Streetsmart managers make sure to establish an environment where good ideas don't have to go to an off-site retreat in order to be recognized.

Making Management Your Business

They're out there. In the diverse and growing landscape of nonprofit organizations, there are outstanding organizations that appear to carry out routine administrative and financial tasks effortlessly, or at least without external signs of stress. These organizations are as notable for their lack of internal crises as they are for the quality of their programs. You probably know at least one or two. You may even be lucky enough to work for one.

These groups span the entire nonprofit sector, from child care programs to mental health centers, from museums to private schools. They can be found in just about every city and region, and they all approach the mundane tasks of management with a comparable level of professional effectiveness.

Why are they important? Because a good deal of the nonprofit sector's efficiency will hinge on their success.

A SHARED RESPONSE TO ENVIRONMENTAL SHIFTS

One of the subtle changes in the nonprofit sector in recent years is the increased level of management expertise. It may not seem that way to most people, because so many nonprofits are small in size and because there has been such a dramatic increase in the number of new nonprofits being formed. Small or start-up organizations usually struggle managerially, and there are so many of them that it gives the illusion that all are struggling.

But there are large and distinct pockets of management excellence in the nonprofit sector. These are typically organizations that have been operating for at least a decade or more, and have developed effective administrative and managerial systems. And it is these centers of excellence around which nonprofits will cluster in the coming years. The reason can be summed up in a single word: *economics*.

Consider the standard administrative duties that must be performed for any nonprofit to stay in operation: payroll production, financial accounting, budget management, site maintenance, office management, equipment procurement and maintenance. All of these routine tasks require specialized knowledge. Many also require specialized equipment, which is often very expensive.

Specialization costs money. It requires significant investments in personnel and equipment, and the ability to maintain those investments over time. Only certain nonprofits ever develop the resources to accomplish this objective. This isn't the same as saying that only well-endowed agencies can develop the resources, because the will and the vision of management is ultimately more important than the balance sheet.

Along with specialization comes management sophistication. Nonprofits in most areas are boosting their level of professional management exponentially. University-based graduate programs are booming, and people with for-profit management credentials are more readily entering the field—it's no accident that two of the last nine United Ways we worked with have a former banker as CEO or a high-ranking executive.

THE C.O.R.E. MODEL

We developed the C.O.R.E. Continuum of Collaboration, shown on the next page, to guide nonprofit collaboration activities of this kind. This model suggests that nonprofits can collaborate on four levels of activity: Corporate (governance and executive management); Operations (programs and services); Responsibility (administrative and financial systems); and Economics (purchasing). Nonprofits can choose to collaborate on all levels or some combination of them.

The kind of nonprofit agencies we are describing have succeeded particularly well on the Responsibility and Economic levels and now are poised to expand on that success beyond the traditional borders of a single agency.

The way they expand on their success is by challenging conven-

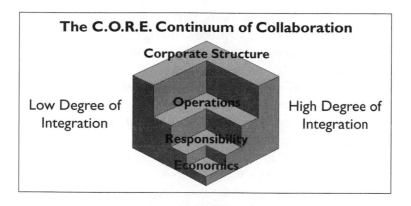

The C.O.R.E. Continuum of Collaboration

Corporate Structure

Low Degree of Integration

Operations

High Degree of Integration

Responsibility

Economics

tional ideas of what a nonprofit agency is supposed to do. These groups continue to be successful in delivering program services, but they also develop what is effectively a subspecialty in the practice of management itself. They do things like create and maintain a city-wide computer network for themselves and their peers, or negotiate health benefits on behalf of a regional buying group. They create and operate marketing programs for themselves and others, arrange for joint purchasing of professional services, and produce paychecks for themselves and a group of other nonprofits.

They do all these things not only because they are natural leaders but in many cases because they are the only ones capable of this type of management sophistication. Smaller, newer or less accomplished nonprofits often lack the resources to develop this level of expertise and frequently resort to using less costly, less reliable systems.

LOWERING THE BARRIERS

This kind of collaboration is happening right now, very quietly, in many different areas. It is not necessarily given any particular label nor even widely discussed. But it will eventually be inevitable as nonprofits cope with the changing economics of service provision in the twenty-first century.

Agencies that are capable of providing administrative services to others must first recognize that they have a specialty others need. This is likely to happen only as the result of a highly entrepreneurial CEO or a careful strategic planning process. Associations of nonprofits may be able to facilitate the emergence of these entities, but few associations have the capacity to provide the services themselves. For-profit organizations seldom have the interest or the ability to provide such services, so these self-selected agencies must find ways of developing their own capacities. To hasten the formation of these collaborative relationships, several things need to happen.

Distinguish between mergers and administrative service provision. Many nonprofits fully realize that one or more of their peer agencies could supply them with administrative services but they equate that with a merger and therefore reject the entire concept. The C.O.R.E. model clearly illustrates that administrative collaboration is *not* the same thing as a merger. Still, there will need to be some mutual education to dispel the idea that providing administrative and financial services to another agency is the same thing as swallowing it up.

Expand the use of technology. No agency can provide administrative services without solid information-processing technology systems. Agencies wishing to develop this subspecialty will need to make major investments in technology and the personnel to manage and operate it.

Accept administrative and financial services as necessary. Many nonprofit administrators and their funding sources still act as though spending money on administration is somehow illicit. Laudable as that sentiment may seem, it is self-defeating in the long run. Our recent analysis of administrative spending in one statewide group of agencies suggests that those who spend too little have management problems as readily as those who spend too much. Nonprofits that emerge as administrative service providers will understand how to balance reasonable administrative spending with high-quality program services.

Devise workable models. Nonprofits that provide superior administrative service in addition to program services are devising new structures and ways of relating to their peers. While the expected benefits are clear enough, the exact vehicles and corporate relationships are just beginning to become clear. The rule here is that the nature of the expected benefits should determine the legal structure of the collaboration, not vice versa.

In the nonprofit sector, innovation has traditionally happened mainly in the delivery of programs and services. Today, innovation is occurring in management techniques as well. Many nonprofits are emerging as administrative service providers for their peers, largely because they are the only groups with sufficient expertise to meet the need. In the process, these organizations with a subspecialty in nonprofit management are boosting the sector's productivity.

The Iron Triangle

The nursing home administrator was feeling good about the results of the state inspection as she motioned the inspector to a chair in her office at the end of the tour. "Any problems?" she asked. "Holes in the cubicle curtains," the inspector said, referring to the plastic curtains that could be drawn around each patient's bed for a measure of privacy.

"Oh, no," said the administrator. "You must be mistaken. Those curtains are all in excellent shape."

The inspector shook his head. "You *should* have holes in the cubicle curtains. At the top, in the mesh near the ceiling. It's a new part of the code."

The administrator was shocked. The inspector, it turned out, was absolutely right. The new regulations required holes in the mesh near the top of each curtain so it would be easier for the sprinkler system's streams of water to get through in case of a fire. The administrator's shock compounded when she had to order new curtains with the specially designed holes and was presented with the $4900 bill for new cubicle curtains. *With holes.*

Media talk about waste in state government gets carried out in a kind of shorthand language with examples like wasteful consulting contracts and screw drivers that cost hundreds of dollars. But once the dialogue gets beyond these convenient, easy-to-understand, and fiscally irrelevant items, it founders. The real issues run deeper than such simple or ideologically correct answers.

The nursing home administrator in this story is part of a phenomenon sometimes called an Iron Triangle, in this case a three-way relationship between a private sector provider of services, a standard-setting branch of government, and a purchasing branch of government. Iron Triangles have their own inescapable logic, as illustrated by the nursing home inspection. Having been told by the standard-setting branch of government to comply at risk of loss of license, the administrator buys the items. Being funded in large measure by government sources, the service provider then requests reimbursement through a more or less formal process. If the additional charge is accepted the provider breathes easier and the government's bill goes up. On the other hand, if the increase is rejected the provider loses the money—at least until it can find a less explicit way of recovering the cost. The major activity of a triangle player, then, is making sure the responsibility for an increase in overall outlay ends up with one of the two other players.

The peculiarly frustrating aspect of the Iron Triangle syndrome is that each transaction, taken on its own, usually seems compelling. In the case of cubicle curtain holes, it evidently is true that a bedridden nursing home patient completely surrounded by cubicle curtains in the midst of a fire with no staff around cannot be protected by the sprinkler system (another Triangle requirement) because the water cannot muster enough velocity to penetrate the dense plastic mesh at the top of the curtains.

What's missing in many individual Iron Triangle situations is a sense of perspective, a sensitivity to the whole. Call it common sense, even. To make things work, one of the players must take a risk. The inspector discovering the curtain faux pas might pretend not to notice, delivering an informal verbal warning of a citation that will come the next time. Or all parties concerned agree to stagger implementation, etc. Unfortunately, the risk of humanizing the process in this way may or may not seem worth taking, so it can never be relied upon. The easiest way out is always to play strictly by the rule book no matter how absurd or impractical the outcome may be.

Part of the solution to the Iron Triangle problem lies in changing who writes the rule books—the standard-setting point of the Triangle. Decades ago, when state government first began purchasing large amounts of health and human services from the private nonprofit sector, the various provider networks were legitimately in their infancy. Government loves to fill a vacuum, especially a noble one, and so it began to take on the responsibility of setting professional and practice standards. The result is that today the purchasing point of the triangle rarely has the authority to demand the level of quality it desires but instead must defer to another branch of the same government—the second point on the Triangle.

At base, this situation is a classic example of responsibility without authority. Like workers on an old-fashioned assembly line each point of the Triangle—purchaser, standard setter, and provider—can honestly say that it controls only part of the whole, a situation ripe for endless buck passing and less than candid public debate.

One of the major reasons why privately initiated and managed standards of practice are so slow to develop in the nonprofit sector is because of this kind of governmental intervention. Virtually all major professions and many industries have private standards-setting capability. Accounting standards are set through national bodies, fire protection codes through a handful of private associations, and numerous crafts are regulated by government bureaus based on private research. Unfortunately, most of the nonprofit service delivery sector has not shown itself capable of replacing governmental entities with self-governance. Until they do, we're all going to have to worry about holes in our curtains.

How to Improve Quality Ten Different Ways

When the gritty television homicide cop leaves the murder scene, viewers know that his veteran mind is already wrestling with one central question: Who had the motive? Once he figures out who had the motive to want the victim gone, our hero will be more than halfway toward figuring out whodunit.

It's the same way with improving quality. Much ink has been spilled in discussing one aspect of quality or another, and it's safe to assume that the volume will only increase in the future. Defining and establishing reliable ways to deliver quality services is a goal that ranks right up there with motherhood and apple pie. The problem is, although we know how to arrange motherhood and bake apple pie, describing and delivering quality services is considerably more difficult. Ignore the fact that in most sectors of the nonprofit field there is no universal definition of quality. Even if there were, we don't have the systems in place to guarantee its delivery. So what can we do?

One approach to answering this question starts with asking who suffers when quality is absent. Who feels the pain when services are provided at below-average quality? Who would therefore have the motive for improving the quality?

One would be tempted to say that funding sources have a motive for improving quality. But do they? The largest single funding source for nonprofit programs is the government—federal, state, and local. Governmental funders are typically under enormous pressure to provide more services rather than better services. One of the reasons government turns to the nonprofit sector is because of its responsiveness. Another is because it is usually cheaper and because it is often easier to just walk away from an underperforming nonprofit than to try to fix the problems. None of these characteristics do much to ensure the quality of the services delivered to users; funders value shorter-term management qualities. While individual officials may sincerely want to build systems of quality care, they have to ignore some fundamental governmental and political realities to do it.

Private philanthropists have an even less compelling way to concern themselves with the quality of services. Individual donors simply don't have the time, interest, or infrastructure they'd need to be sure they're funding quality services. And private foundations are under pressure to distribute minimum percentages of their total assets regardless of whether the funded services are high quality or not. Moreover, few foundations have developed the staff and measurement capabilities necessary to confirm quality in services.

So, who stands to gain from improving the quality of services in the nonprofit sector? What player in the nonprofit world has a strong and lasting incentive to see quality programs developed and delivered by the average nonprofit? Our nomination: your insurance companies.

Look at Table 1. It summarizes some of the common insurance coverages agencies must have in order to provide services responsibly. It shows the type of insurance, the risk it typically covers, and the management areas relevant to the risk. To improve the quality of services, what we need to do is get the weight of insurance coverages behind changes in the areas in the right-hand column.

For example, most workers' compensation claims involve lost time and "soft tissue" injuries (meaning things like torn ligaments and twisted back muscles, not broken bones). Workers' compensation specialists have already demonstrated the link between reduced claims and proper training for employees that must lift as part of their jobs. They've also shown how an inclusionary workforce style helps reduce lost time due to injuries, since injured employees are more likely to return to work in a place that actively asks them to do so. In short, better training programs and more attention to the work environment reduces workers' compensation costs. Not coincidentally, these improvements also help contribute to the quality of services provided.

Table 1. Common Insurance Covering Agencies

Type of Insurance	What's Covered	Area(s) Affected
Workers' compensation	On-the-job injuries and illnesses	Workplace standards, client interactions, qualifications of staff, and employee morale
Commercial automobile insurance	Property and personal injury to others	Transportation-related issues; life safety
Health insurance	Employee health care costs	Human resource management
Life insurance	Employee mortality	Human resource management
Corporate professional liability	Civil actions related to deviations from accepted professional standards	All program delivery systems
Fiduciary responsibility	Benefits and insurance administration	Administrative systems and policies
Property and general liability	Site-related losses and injuries	Site management
Unemployment	Lost wages due to lay-offs	Recruitment practices, hiring and firing policies
Surety bonds (fidelity insurance)	Losses due to embezzlement and employee theft	Internal controls
Directors and officers	Actions arising from duties as board members and executives	Leadership and management decisions

But to say that there is a connection between the interests of the insurance companies and day-to-day nonprofit operations is not enough. There needs to be a clear-cut pathway and a built-in incentive for making quality-based changes.

Ultimately that incentive—not surprisingly—is money. Over time, reduced risk means reduced cost of insurance. (A caveat—this equation applies mainly on an industry basis. It is not necessarily true that an individual nonprofit can reduce insurance costs by reducing its own risk as an individual organization. Insurers prefer big numbers.)

Ironically, the money incentive is not as strong as one might hope. Many of the common insurance coverages listed here simply don't cost enough to get management's attention. For instance, unemployment insurance usually doesn't cost much more than a few hundred dollars per employee. Moreover, many nonprofit managers regard insurance coverage as a nuisance subject that's best avoided or handed off to a helpful insurance agent who's on the board. Too bad; this means missed opportunities.

It's the pathway that holds the promise. By pathway we mean how the nonprofit gets the insurance, and what they have to do in order to keep their access to the coverage. Put simply, if the insurance industry is interested in reducing claims to improve their own profitability, it has at least ten handy levers for making this happen. By raising standards for insurance—or by providing risk management services—the industry has the power to improve everything from the professionalism of service delivery (professional liability insurance) to the way nonprofits treat their employees (unemployment and workers' compensation, although unemployment coverage is more accurately a government "insurance" program).

Another way that changing the pathway can help boost quality standards is through joint insurance purchasing. By collaborating across an entire state or in a specific field of service, nonprofits can help control costs and establish a self-enforcing peer group. Many nonprofits today belong to group buying programs or insurance trusts run by some sort of regional or national association. It's a short step to go from simple membership to proactive management.

Funders and accrediting agencies can also help by paying more attention to this seemingly obscure area of management. A simple look at an agency's record of workers' compensation claims and associated payouts can tell more about the real human resource practices of a nonprofit than a stack of nicely printed human resource policy manuals. The written record of workplace injuries may be far more revealing than anything that a simple site visit could provide.

How to achieve quality services is a subject that will occupy teams of researchers, philosophers, and data analysts for the next several years. In the meantime, we already have some useful information and have established methods for making some real inroads into systemic quality service provision. It would be a crime not to use them.

What Your Funding Sources Want from Managed Care

We once had the opportunity to interview members of a selection team from a state Medicaid department that had just changed its managed behavioral health care company. The results were instructive from several perspectives, the most important of which was that these key representatives of a major payor talked at length about their thinking and reasoning as they decided which competing entity would take their managed care program through the next several years. Although it is important not to infer too much about other payors' desires from a single rebid process, there is also no reason to think that it is likely to be substantially different. And if this experience says anything valid about what other payors want from managed care, then it says something very significant about how other providers will have to respond.

WHAT THE DIVISION SOUGHT

From the beginning of the process it was clear that Medicaid sought four things from a managed care company: lower costs than it was already paying; the willingness and ability on the part of the winning company to assume more risk; demonstrated experience in managing care; and managed care systems that were large enough and sophisticated enough to do the job. We'll take these four items in order.

Lower Costs

Although Medicaid had already reduced its costs substantially through the first managed care contract, officials were convinced that more savings could be wrung from the existing system. They sought lower costs for services provided, and seemed to feel that those savings could come from virtually all aspects of the program. In particular, they felt that administrative costs could go down on a unit basis, arguing that the additional services to be part of the next contract would allow the same or slightly higher administrative costs to be spread over a wider base of services.

More Risk

The next most significant improvement that Medicaid officials were looking for, from their perspective, was the willingness and ability of the winning company to assume more risk. They apparently felt that the previous management company—which bid on the renewal but eventually lost it—were insufficiently at risk to motivate organizational changes. "They could afford to just walk away," said one of the government's team members. The implication was that the design of the original contract was essentially a consulting company engagement, rather than one in which Medicaid and its managed care company shared in both the rewards of success and the risk of failure.

Experience in Managing Behavioral Health Care

Whether it's a government agency issuing a contract for managed care or an individual applying for a job, those responsible for it always look for prior experience. In this case, they wanted to be sure that the individuals involved in the contract had sound experience in managing behavioral health care. This alone narrows the field.

Large and Sophisticated Administrative Systems

Even in the relatively short time that managed care has been a reality, there has been an increase in the sophistication level. Consistent with their focus on experience and the company's willingness and ability to assume more risk, officials wanted to know that their eventual partner had developed sophisticated administrative systems capable of handling large volumes of activity. This meant the ability to do everything from data management and analysis to claims adjudication and in-house staff training.

WHAT IT IMPLIES

At this point readers may be asking why we would focus so much on the relationship between a government payor and its for-profit managed care company. What difference do the details of this type of negotiation make? The answer is straightforward. *What payors demand of their managed care contractors is what those contractors will demand of their service providers, and most of those providers are nonprofit agencies.*

Start with lower costs. Payors' appetite for lower costs is going to be insatiable. In our case study, the previous managed care company had made major savings yet the government payor was convinced that more were achievable. They pressured the contractor for more savings knowing full well that the pressure would be transmitted to the providers because, in essence, it is the managed care company's job to transmit that pressure through its various policies and systems.

One of the implications of the desire for contractors to bear more risk is obvious, but the others are more subtle. The obvious one is that managed care companies are going to be looking for provider partners willing and able to share that risk. This is obvious to anyone who has followed the growth of managed care, and is now taken for granted.

The other implication follows naturally. Ultimately it is the managed care company that stands between the payor and the provider. The biggest risk is theirs. When the scope of the project reaches into the hundreds of millions of dollars, the amounts at risk—even if they're only a small percentage of the total—can easily total millions. Consequently, managed care companies will generally need to have deep pockets and the tolerance for large financial risks.

This suggests that provider-based networks will never likely be primary risk-takers in a managed care environment. Instead, their risk will be largely confined to the vagaries of service provision for a sliver of the overall population. Moreover, there will be a limited number of managed care companies that will be capable of such risk levels, which in turn implies that a proportionately small number of companies will get the majority of the managed care contracts.

To survive under conditions of high risk and to stretch their administrative allocation, the companies will limit the numbers of providers with whom they do business. This happened a few years ago when a national insurance company announced plans to trim the total number of home health care providers it did business with from 200 to *three*. With fewer providers to provide the full scope of services to a given managed care population, each group will have to be able to cover the full range of service types. This is what will turn the universally cited model of a continuum of care from a half-hearted goal into an operational reality.

FOR THE REST OF US

This example happens to have been in behavioral health care, but its lessons are equally valid for any field which faces managed care. What's more, in the future we're likely to see other payors adopt the same stance once managed care leaves its mark on the health care field. Corrections, for example, is an area that is prime for a restructuring along these lines, as is education at all levels.

The thing to keep in mind is that managed care will look different in virtually every setting where it is tried. Managed care in the hospital and doctor's office gets the most attention, but most funders are trying or have tried to implement their own brand of managed care. Standardized testing, for example, is the education world's equivalent of a part of managed care. Level funding from government funders is a crude form of managed care: The outcome orientations that some United Way agencies are exploring are also a form of managing services. Once the technology and best administrative practices of managing care are more formalized and easier to pass on, it is conceivable that it will become the mode of choice in purchasing services of virtually all kinds from nonprofit providers. Wise managers will do well to read the early lessons.

The Core Competence of the Nonprofit Corporation

From hospitals and universities to art museums and day care centers, nonprofit organizations are facing increased demand for services. The positive side is that most can weather this period by a single-minded focus on an organizing principle of uncommon potency.

Called *core competence,* this is an idea developed in the literature by C.K. Prahalad and Gary Hamel. It can be defined as the collective learning of a corporation about coordinating diverse skills in the delivery of an irreducible service, and although most of its roots are in the for-profit sector, it applies equally well in nonprofit settings. The collective learning aspect of an organization's core competence is especially important in nonprofit corporations because although it rests on the knowledge of the employees, the corporation's core competence does not reside exclusively in one or two individuals. Nor is it dependent on such ultimately transient things as technology or capital investment. Rather, it exists in the delicate mix of all these elements as preserved and directed by management.

The classic example of a durable and pervasive core competence is the Sony Corporation. To the casual observer Sony appears to be merely an electronics corporation, albeit a good one. But what the organization really does best is miniaturization. Its people, technology, systems, and management approach are all woven together in the service of the same overriding goal.

Successful nonprofit organizations organize themselves in exactly the same fashion, although not necessarily as consciously. I know of one teaching hospital in a medium-sized community that appears on the surface to be a traditional medical facility. Yet its original organizing papers did not say a single word about the corporation they were establishing being a hospital. Instead, they specified that the mission was providing health care to the poor, and over the years that was exactly what they had done. This persistent sense of a core competence showed up in elements as diverse as their geographic location and the controller's endless creativity in finding ways to make the reimbursement system work for poor patients, not against them.

Another group I know appears to be a hopeless hodgepodge of services and programs. Their central offices always appear to be in chaos, and managers seem to invent policies and procedures for the moment. Yet the agency is financially sound, the staff happy and secure, and their services respected. The reason is simple: Their core competence is dealing with people in emergencies. This is the unifying theme that runs through all they do, and they have quite deliberately organized themselves to be a central part of virtually all non-medical emergencies in their city.

Core competencies meet three standards. First, they allow access to a wide variety of public needs. In fact, understanding a nonprofit organization's core competence can be truly a liberating, uplifting experience. The struggling Big Brother/Big Sister agency, for example, could instantly expand its service potential simply by recognizing that its core competence is essentially that of a broker, and that this basic organizational ability soon will be far more in demand than ever before. Second, the recipients of the service—or the funding source—must regard it as a thing of value. Third—and this is where the nonprofit corporation's core competence differs from its proprietary counterpart's—it must be replicable. Since most nonprofit organizations do not generally employ patented technology, and since there is a substantial obligation of public service in the nonprofit charter, replicability is essential if the competence is to be meaningful.

Prahalad's and Hamel's insight is that core competencies form the basis for competitiveness. By contrast, a nonprofit organization's core competence is the basis for its unique contribution to the public good. While it is in the best interests of competitive private business to protect competitive advantage by keeping one's core competencies shrouded in as much operational mystery as possible, the non-profit's public charter implies a responsibility to act on behalf of the greater good.

Happily, the shared nature of core competencies in the nonprofit sector usually results in an overall improvement in society's learning about how to deal with a problem or need. This is why such diverse activities as caring for AIDS patients and operating community residences for the mentally retarded have seen so much improvement at the operational level in recent years. Core competencies in the nonprofit sector benefit us all.

A Different Kind of Growth

Used to be, the path to growth was pretty clear. If you already offered a certain kind of service and wanted to grow, you looked around for an opportunity to expand it. That opportunity might come through a foundation grant, a government request for proposals, a special pilot project, a simple expansion of services by adding more staff, or any one of a variety of other ways.

On the other hand, if it was a new service you needed to be a bit more creative. Sometimes those same funding sources would take a chance on a good plan for delivering a related service. Sometimes, especially in the 1960s and 1970s, government organizations were so desperate for nonprofit partners that simply being in the right place at the right time was almost enough.

Either way, growth came through program services. The folks who ran the programs—from halfway houses to hospitals to museums and schools—always sat in the captain's chair when it came to growing the agency.

This is still the preferred way of achieving growth, and rightfully so. Nonprofits exist to pursue a mission, and they fulfill it by providing services. But some organizations are discovering that there is another way to grow. It is far more diverse than traditional program services, offers different rewards, and demands a different mindset. For lack of a better term, we'll call these areas administrative and management services. Here are three examples of actual agencies' growth initiatives in these areas.

Transportation and Fleet Maintenance. This social service agency providing a wide array of services to mentally retarded and developmentally delayed individuals was required by its funding source to assume responsibility for transporting clients from one program to another. In a fairly short time it had assembled all the components of a modest corporate fleet: vehicles, storage and repair facilities, and support staff.

Transportation services is one of those areas most susceptible to brute economic force, and it wasn't long before smaller organizations in the same field found the costs of maintaining small numbers of vehicles prohibitive. One or two began contracting with their much larger sister agency, and today over a third of the vehicles the larger organization services are brought to them via fleet maintenance contracts.

Insurance. A residential services agency employed hundreds of people in entry-level and near-entry-level positions. Realizing the sheer bulk of employees in a single job category, as well as the numbers represented by similar agencies in the same geographic area, the organization initiated a self-insurance plan for unemployment insurance. The usual short-term gains that a new insurance plan enjoys were helped along by an improving local economy and declining unemployment. After only a few years, the plan was serving almost twenty comparable agencies, saving all of them money over the rates they would have previously paid.

Real estate maintenance services. A large provider of residential and workshop services was acutely aware of its investment in the tools of the real estate maintenance trade. These ranged from lawn mowers to carpentry tools and the staff to operate them. When a nearby smaller provider experienced serious problems with one of its residences they began to help. Today the only thing limiting the contracts they sign with other agencies to manage property is their willingness to invest time and money in the effort.

There is nothing exotic about any of the above projects. Hundreds of thousands of nonprofits around the country already have all or most of what they need in order to provide the same kind of services. What they lack is mainly the encouragement to pursue a previously unexplored path. Let this chapter provide that initial push (if you are a financial manager or you handle all the agency's vans, maybe that's why this excerpt ended up on your desk).

Nonprofits successful in this way tend to think differently than most other agencies. They are constantly looking for ways to grow, and they have a clear grasp of the economics of their organization. It is this different way of thinking that helps them see opportunities where others see only dull necessity. As an entity they know how to capitalize on special assets, and they can recognize and promote unique abilities on the part of staffs.

Of course, agencies need a few other things too. Here are a few pointers:

Size helps. What all these organizations above have in common is that they are large nonprofits, meaning over $10 million in annual revenue. They have a skilled and adequately staffed management team that is willing to take risks, and boards that will support them. They are also financially sound. No one can think innovatively when the next round of payroll checks might bounce.

Look for volume. Organizations tend to get good at things they do a lot. One would expect that some of the greatest accomplishments in the growth of management and administrative services would come in human resource functions, since personnel tends to be the single largest expenditure of most nonprofits.

Find the pain. Every one of these successful ventures started out with the initiating agency feeling some pain. Nonprofits with large numbers of residential programs must be good at managing property or else the programs can literally fall apart. Insurance for nonprofits can often be a problem, as can managing a fleet of motor vehicles. Each of the agencies found ways to become accomplished in these areas and then recognized that what was a problem for them was probably a problem for others too. The logical conclusion was to share their expertise.

Ignore the jargon. In the early stages, if anyone had suggested that fleet maintenance and transportation services were an appropriate area of expansion for a nonprofit, many in the agency would have recoiled from the idea. Yet they now run one of the largest commercial fleets in their geographic area. How? They simply focused on a problem and then offered their solution to others.

Serve other nonprofits. No one nonprofit can be all things to all people. Our successful agencies chose, for a variety of reasons, to focus on one or two areas in which they could be successful and then they offered that success to their peers.

The benefits of growth through administrative and management services are numerous. Some, such as simple profitability and the creation of new revenue streams are obvious. Others are a bit more subtle. For one, profit generated through management and administrative services may be out of reach for government funding sources that might be tempted to lay claim to it if it were traditional fundraising in support of programs for which they contract. Growth through management and administrative services can also be pleasantly challenging for managers who might otherwise get stuck in a rut. This can help recruit and retain good management staff.

Most subtle of all is the way growth through management and administrative services improves a nonprofit's strategic position. Most observers of social and health care services believe that there are too many nonprofits providing services in different areas around the country, and that managed care or a similar effort will eventually reduce these numbers. When that happens, only a handful of agencies are likely to emerge as the core of regionally strong merged entities or alliances. What better way of positioning for that future role than to begin providing management and administrative systems today?

Three minor disadvantages. First, profitability in services not directly related to a charity's tax exempt mission can mean it has to pay taxes, or Unrelated Business Income Tax (UBIT). So what? UBIT is really a sign of success, and as long as the business doesn't threaten the tax exempt status of the agency (which is unlikely anyway), managers needn't worry about paying their fair share of taxes on unrelated profit.

Second, some will argue that providing management and administrative services could create unfair competition with for-profit, taxable entities. If carried to an extreme this may be the case—but the outlines of entrepreneurial strategies presented here are not likely to rise to that level.

Third, this kind of growth demands management time and energy and can divert attention from the mission if not managed properly. The agency needs to have people with the right skills in place before even considering this direction, and it must have decent management systems and some good managers on the bench. In the end, however, these are relatively minor considerations that shouldn't distract from a focus on growing in new and innovative ways.

Collaborating to Compete

Independently, two nonprofit boards were contemplating a paradox. As leaders in their geographic area, they had investigated the possibility of merging with each other but for various reasons had decided against it. In fact, they had each decided to pursue distinctly different courses that would inevitably put them into direct competition at some point in the future. Now they were being asked to consider a riddle: the more they competed, the more they would have to collaborate.

The two nonprofits each had long and respected histories of service to mentally retarded and developmentally disabled individuals (MR/DD). They were by far the two largest such service providers of the nearly fifty in the area. Their array of services was comparable, and they had competed for the same funding on many occasions.

In part, the merger had not worked because each agency had independently designed a strategy that could reasonably be expected to lead to mergers with some of the smaller agencies within a few years. One of the groups had established a self-insured worker's compensation program that had met with so much success that over a dozen other agencies had been invited to join it. They were planning to expand that same model to a variety of administrative services, thereby creating a management services organization (MSO).

The other agency took a different approach. They had convened a group of smaller organizations in the mental retardation/developmental disabilities services field and offered to provide each with targeted forms of management assistance at no charge. Senior managers of the agency would be responsible for spending some time at each member's offices analyzing the agency and offering solutions to their most pressing problems.

Neither agency explicitly labeled its program for collaboration a prelude to merger; in fact, the first agency rejected that characterization altogether. Still, it was not unreasonable to expect that, eventually, many of the smaller providers would need to and want to merge with one of the larger agencies in the area—and when the time came, who better to consider than an already existing partner?

The boards could understand the notion of competition as it related to the two large agencies, and both agencies' plans for reaching out to others were clearly types of collaboration. But what they could not understand was that the competitive path on which they had now decided to embark was going to lead them, ironically, in the direction of more collaboration with each other as well.

The idea of competition between nonprofits, though it is becoming more commonplace, is foreign and distasteful to some. It conjures up images of cutthroat price wars, corporate bankruptcies, and business people with dubious ethics. But the nature of competition in the nonprofit world is very different.

First, consider the nature of ordinary consumer competition. Ford, GM, and Daimler-Chrysler are the only three big domestic car makers. Along with foreign car companies, they compete for literally millions of customers. With that size market it is quite possible to focus on hundreds of different car-buying segments, designing low cost vehicles to appeal to large numbers of people or high priced products for very small groups.

Most health and human service providers, however, have almost the exact reverse situation. Instead of a handful of suppliers and a large number of buyers, there is only one buyer (government) and a large number of sellers. That was the case with the two agencies who operated in a marketplace of fifty, with only one real buyer—state government.

In the consumer world, regulators worry a lot about monopolies—a number of buyers at the mercy of one supplier. Many nonprofits face a monopsony—many suppliers at the mercy of one buyer. Just as in monopolies, that buyer holds tremendous power over the suppliers, as anyone who has ever been part of a state government-funded system knows.

As a consequence, competition is different. Rather than being open-ended and measured by things like total revenue and share of

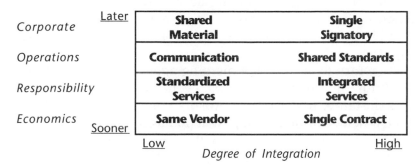

Figure 5. Continuums of Collaboration

the total market, competition in the nonprofit world tends to resemble competition between two departments in the same large bureaucracy. It can become every bit as fierce, but ultimately the parties have more common interests—such as the continued survival of the monopsonist—than not.

Collaboration is also easier and more likely. To illustrate why, look at Figure 5, a slightly different version of the C.O.R.E. continuum earlier.

This chart shows how collaboration is really a matter of continuums. Economics is always the easiest common ground on which to collaborate, the low-hanging fruit of collaboration. Exchanging information about purchasing patterns, good vendors, and favorable prices offers low-integration economic collaboration. If five agencies got together to buy a year's worth of copier paper, hired a storage facility to warehouse it, and devised a way to distribute it among themselves, it would still be economic collaboration, but of a highly integrated nature. Simply agreeing to use the same basic office software applications is a low-integration way of standardizing services on the responsibility level of the continuum. Developing a wide-area network with common ownership of the software used is a high-integration form of working together.

Operations collaboration can be as simple as, say, arranging for staff to attend the same training sessions together. At the high end, when organizations commit to a common set of service definitions and a standard way of providing the same services, it makes for a more highly integrated type of collaboration. Finally, doing joint marketing is a relatively low-integration form of corporate collaboration, but agreeing on a single signatory usually requires either a full merger or a legally binding service delivery alliance. When agencies collaborate on any one or all three of the lower three levels, we call it an alliance. When they collaborate on all four levels, it's a merger.

Let's return to our two nonmerging agencies. Collaboration is in their future in a number of ways, even if they may not recognize it. For instance, managed care (or its equivalent) is touching the MR/DD field. One of the things that managed care demands is common standards of care. Payers will eventually demand that community residential programs uphold the same standards, that supported employment programs be carried out with the same general performance levels, etc.

What more logical leaders in the local effort to standardize services on the operations level than our two agencies? The same would be true for information exchange standards on the responsibility level, which will also be needed in the service system of the future. In fact, right now it would be possible for them and only a handful of other organizations to take the lead in designing technical and programmatic information standards to take effect in three or four years. This is what it means to be proactive, and it can *only* be accomplished collaboratively.

There are three characteristics of nonprofit competition that make it different from what we are used to in the for-profit environment.

1. The push toward competition usually originates from outside the organization. Nonprofits are not inherently competitive organizations. Their financial and legal structure deliberately does not lend itself to traditional marketplace competition. When nonprofits become competitive, it is typically because external conditions push them in that direction. Reduced governmental funding in many areas and the advent of managed care in the health field are good examples of outside forces creating a competitive environment for nonprofits. In our two agencies, it was the prospect of changes in the reimbursement system that prompted them to explore a merger in the first place. One reason why the merger was rejected was because the external pressure in that direction had yet to reach compelling proportions.

2. Done properly, competition between nonprofits can benefit society. Analyze the approaches to collaboration of the two agencies. Each initiative is different in style and approach, but they share a common characteristic: *The overall service system will be stronger if it* *succeeds.* If both approaches work—and this is not an unreasonable expectation—many other agencies will be strengthened.

The same is true for full mergers. When any nonprofit becomes too weak to carry out its mission, society suffers for it. This is why early mergers in any area tend to involve a strong and a weak partner, while later ones tend to match strength with strength.

3. Collaboration is inevitable. To survive, even competitors must collaborate. Many nonprofit managers are beginning to accept the necessity for being more competitive in the service of their mission. The next step is to understand how to collaborate at the same time. Future competitors will have a greater stake in learning how to collaborate precisely because they will be more competitive. The idea that nonprofits must begin to collaborate is not an idealistic feel-good assertion, but the natural outcome of forces presently at work, including the trend toward greater competitiveness. Competition can strengthen agencies. Ironically, it can also strengthen the bonds between them.

The Power of
Social Enterprise

Seeking to fund programs and serve clients, most nonprofit organizations trying to reach beyond a steady diet of governmental and foundation funding turn to individual fundraising and planned giving efforts. The mechanics of these three revenue streams are often quite different, but one thing they have in common is that they make the nonprofit profoundly reactive. The wealth that each offers is created and maintained outside the nonprofit, so the nonprofit's managers must first discern the stated tastes and ideologies of the givers and then design a proposal to match.

This is not as easy as it sounds, since the interests and preferences of the givers may not match up with the needs of the service recipients. The nonprofit is then caught in the middle, constantly trying to tailor its pitch to the funders while coping with the true needs of the clients. Most nonprofit managers and board members will recognize this as one of the classic tensions in the field.

SOCIAL ENTERPRISE

A small but rapidly growing number of nonprofit agencies are exploring a new model of both funding and service provision that answers these questions in a bold and innovative way. At the moment, what they are doing is called social enterprise, which seems as good a term as any in this rapidly evolving field. It's also called community wealth creation, social purpose businesses, venture philanthropy, and probably other things as well. And if a loose network of practitioners in the field is any guide, there is enough energy and enthusiasm behind the movement for it to leave a major mark on all nonprofits, not just the ones engaging explicitly in the practice.

What is a social enterprise? It is a blending of business and traditional social service that attempts to use the best of both models for the benefit of clients. Here are some examples:

Road to Responsibility, a provider of services to mentally retarded and developmentally disabled individuals, which bought a motel in bankruptcy, reorganized it and currently operates it by employing its own clients.

Larkin Business Ventures, a youth services provider that operated a Ben & Jerry's Ice Cream franchise, a concession at San Francisco's 3Com Park, a special events catering business, and other enterprises employing their social service clients.

Rubicon Programs, Inc., a multiservice provider that has operated a retail nursery, a buildings and grounds maintenance service, and a bakery and catering business. All of these ventures drew as employees clients of the agency's traditional social service programs.

TYPES OF SOCIAL ENTERPRISES

The Roberts Foundation in San Francisco has been particularly active in funding community wealth creation activities in its service area, as well as researching and documenting them. They have identified five distinct types of social enterprises:

Open market services in which the social enterprise competes against all other providers of the service. RTR and certain Larkin enterprises are in this category.

Franchise operations such as Larkin's Ben & Jerry's ice cream ventures. In this case, nonprofits' enterprises are essentially no different from any other franchisee's programs.

Sheltered services such as Rubicon Building and Grounds that operate with the assistance of such set-asides as the National Industries for the Severely Handicapped, an intermediary assisting nonprofits that are encouraged to supply products and services to the federal government.

Program-based enterprises that grow directly from the programs and services of a traditional social service organization.

Cooperatives, a commonly owned corporation through which workers control at least some of the business in addition to being paid by it.

What all of these social enterprises have in common is that at least some of the wealth they use is internally generated, that is, produced by providing a product or service for which some sort of consumer pays money directly. This is what makes the transaction much more direct and immediate than traditional government or foundation funding.

WHAT IT TAKES

Unlike traditional development activities and most government funding programs, both of which are highly formalized or heavily regulated, social enterprise is almost literally wide open. Virtually all social enterprises are highly unique although, ironically, few of the components are new or unique in themselves. The novelty lies in the packaging, the blending of formerly disconnected aspects of traditional social service and standard business practices. To the extent that it is possible to generalize about such an emerging and hard-to-categorize field, the Roberts Foundation and the practitioners it supports identify a handful of must-haves.

A commitment from leadership. The CEO must set an entrepreneurial tone throughout the agency, encouraging and even insisting on participation and some level of buy-in from everyone.

Acceptance of change. It doesn't take much organizational change to submit yet another foundation proposal, or to start up another government-funded program. But an entrepreneurial venture will demand an unusual amount of change, if only because it will force the sponsoring entity to execute hard-core business judgments.

Management sophistication. Small or unsophisticated organizations can easily stumble in entrepreneurial ventures, whether they are nonprofit or for-profit.

Good advisors. Similarly, few organizations of any kind have all the requisite knowledge already employed on staff. The ability to recognize and recruit good advisors is the only viable substitute.

Access to capital. Since they are unable to sell ownership shares to raise capital, nonprofits must find creative alternatives to traditional sources of capital.

IDENTIFY CORE COMPETENCIES FIRST

Any entrepreneur will agree that a successful venture must be rooted in what an individual or company knows best. In the case of a nonprofit, that means that planning a social enterprise starts with a realistic assessment of the organization's core competencies. These are the services that are at the heart of a program, and that are built into the whole way of doing things rather than being the specialty of just one individual.

Most health and human service providers have mastered at least a few core competencies just to stay in business. For instance, many programs have to feed people, while others must keep clients safe at vulnerable times, such as sleeping hours. These may not be glamorous activities but they are necessary, and without the ability to perform them well day after day an agency won't stay in business.

Those same competencies get repackaged and sold every day by for-profit organizations. Entrepreneurial nonprofits recognize this and carve out a market in which to offer their services just like any other service-providing entity. This is why so many nonprofits getting into social enterprises pick restaurants or catering businesses or other aspects of the hospitality field. Their systems are already in place, the staff know how to carry out the activity, and the clients themselves can learn transferable skills.

Beyond the ability to read the market and identify opportunities, socially enterprising nonprofits have to be able to serve *two* bottom lines. The first is the widely understood financial bottom line, the one that prompts an organization to start up a venture in the first place. Equally important is the sense that causes an organization to avoid or get out of an unwise business proposition. The second bottom line is client service. This is the one that holds service to the agency mission as the topmost priority. It is the one that truly keeps a nonprofit's social enterprise from looking like any other ice cream franchise. In the end, it is the most important line of all.

NOT A GRANT REPLACEMENT DEVICE

Community wealth creation programs should never be considered a replacement for government service contracts or foundation grants. For a variety of valid reasons, they will not replace the development office. Instead, they should be viewed as another tool in the smart manager's kit. Many of the principles behind these kinds of programs can apply equally well in traditional social service and health care programs. More important, a successful venture will have agency-wide educational and motivational effects. Not every nonprofit manager is going to be a social entrepreneur. But every nonprofit manager can learn to think a little bit like one.

Needed: Clearly Marked Exits

An agitated woman stands in the lobby of the state attorney general's office. She needs to know how to close down her nonprofit organization, and she thinks she's getting the run-around. No, the official behind the counter tells her, it's not a run-around. To close down a nonprofit you really have to do all of these things. He goes through the list of steps once more. It's not a long list, but matters of geography, time, finance, and legal requirements mean that it's going to take more effort than she expected. Frustrated, she stands silently, considering her options.

Battered by Medicare cuts and the rapidly changing nature of the health care system, a home health agency has decided to turn their operations over to a large regional hospital in the hopes of saving the services. The problem is, they can't execute the strategy. To turn their operations over to the hospital properly requires the assistance of paid professional advisors and a lot of staff time, neither of which they have right now. And the hospital itself, attempting to cope with its own challenges, can't afford to subsidize the effort.

These two dilemmas illustrate a little-appreciated but profoundly important truth of nonprofit management: *There is no exit.* A combination of legal, financial, political, and psychosocial factors means that the doorway leading out of business for nonprofit organizations is shut and bolted from the outside. Not completely unpassable, perhaps, but tight enough that it takes persistence and ingenuity to get through it. And this fact has major consequences for nonprofits and for the public that they exist to serve.

MULTIPLE REASONS

The reasons for this situation are multiple and varied. The legal basis of nonprofits is the starting point. Conceptually, a nonprofit is supposed to be tied up tightly enough that the assets it receives for its quasi-public purposes don't leak into private hands. That's why a state's grant of tax exempt status to an organization requires that any assets remaining after liquidation must pass on to some other comparable organization rather than into a private individual's pockets.

This is also why people say that nonprofits are supposed to "put the money back into the programs." Except for salaries and other expenses, that money isn't supposed to get out at all. This is why economists call nonprofits *capital traps*. Money flows in, but, unlike for-profits, it can't flow back out as dividends or profits. Rightfully, the door is bolted for capital.

Another reason why the door is barred to entire organizations is because there is no exit criteria in nonprofits. Given poor enough performance over a long enough period of time, a for-profit organization's owners will inevitably close it down. Poor performance for for-profits means no profit and little chance of making one in the future. But profit isn't a standard by which outsiders judge nonprofits, and as long as a nonprofit can keep finding even a few revenue sources it has no motivation to head for the exits.

There are psychological reasons too. Agencies often identify fiercely with the local community, and vice versa. Community pride is likely to take a bigger hit if a local art museum closes than if a manufacturer with the same number of employees goes out of business. There are economic incentives for nonprofits to try to stay in business. Without a profit motive and with no agreed-upon standard of programmatic success, the market doesn't know how to punish a nonprofit for failing. Executives and managers in such an environment can enjoy a great deal of staying power.

SECTOR GROWTH, SECTOR FRAGMENTATION

The lack of accepted exits for nonprofits has multiple implications. In part it accounts for the dramatic growth in the sheer number of nonprofits founded since the 1980s. Although it is true that nonprofits have been created to respond to new and different needs, the more compelling explanation is that the exit door is closed for most of them. More are being added, but few are being subtracted.

The lack of exits as an acceptable part of nonprofit management explains the fragmentation of the nonprofit industry. As strategist Michael Porter has written, "If there are exit barriers, marginal firms will tend to stay in the industry and thereby hold back consolidation." True, many nonprofits prefer to remain intensely local in nature and manage to do so quite nicely. Moreover, there is a strong argument to be made for a large number of community-based agencies in certain circumstances. But irresistible environmental forces are broadening the definition of "community." This is exactly what has happened to hospitals, mental health centers, home health agencies, and other health care providers that have been forced to serve a wider area just to stay competitive. Other types of nonprofits are not far behind.

With no exits and a lagging commitment to technology, nonprofits trap people as well as capital. When this means adding an extra staff person to give clients more personal attention, it's perfectly appropriate. But when it means the business office needs five people to keep the financial records instead of four people plus a computer system, it is a waste of resources masquerading as frugality. It also means that there will always be downward pressure on workers' wages because new money coming in must go to support the latest venture instead of paying existing staff better.

THE RESPONSE

As usual, the cheapest and most powerful response to this riddle is a change in thinking. Our friend in the attorney general's office notwithstanding, the steepest barriers to nonprofit exits are psychological rather than procedural. Board members, managers, and funders need to begin to accept the idea of rational exits for existing nonprofits. Removing the stigma from nonprofits that choose to restructure will help unbolt the door.

Foundations could be particularly instrumental in this shift, especially since traditional grants-giving practices have historically encouraged forming new nonprofits as a major strategy for solving many problems. Why not switch some of those start-up funds to wind-down efforts? It would be far less glamorous, of course, but if foundations concentrated in this area they may actually find that they achieve a proportionately greater impact than if they had funded another ten projects of the same kind.

Another relatively simple device is to begin including a discussion of exit strategies in routine strategic planning efforts. It may be painful to contemplate, and it certainly is almost an unnatural activity, but a true fiduciary duty requires it. Even if agencies don't include an explicit exit strategy, at least a general discussion of the circumstances under which the organization will close down or restructure would help.

PART FOUR

Organizational Structure

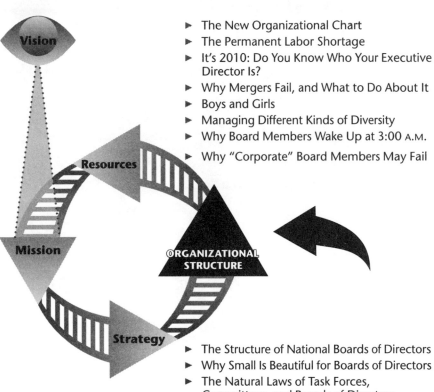

- ▶ The New Organizational Chart
- ▶ The Permanent Labor Shortage
- ▶ It's 2010: Do You Know Who Your Executive Director Is?
- ▶ Why Mergers Fail, and What to Do About It
- ▶ Boys and Girls
- ▶ Managing Different Kinds of Diversity
- ▶ Why Board Members Wake Up at 3:00 A.M.
- ▶ Why "Corporate" Board Members May Fail

- ▶ The Structure of National Boards of Directors
- ▶ Why Small Is Beautiful for Boards of Directors
- ▶ The Natural Laws of Task Forces, Committees, and Boards of Directors
- ▶ In Praise of Hidden Government Subsidies
- ▶ The Rise of the ASO
- ▶ Proactive Management through Benchmarking
- ▶ Giving Diligence Its Due
- ▶ Related Parties
- ▶ Down With Geography, or Why You Have Service Gaps
- ▶ Rethinking the United Way
- ▶ Gilt by Association: Why Associations Must Reshape Themselves
- ▶ The Business of Trade Shows

The New
Organizational Chart

Managers and their ilk have certain *comfort tools*, things which prove useful in recurring situations. We use these comfort tools because they are widely recognized and fill a purpose time after time. Resumes are a good example of a comfort tool. So are job descriptions.

We use the term comfort tool to emphasize their role in giving managers reassurance that they are dealing with a more or less familiar situation. This distinguishes them from more rigidly proscribed management tools such as financial statements, whose content and formats are determined by a third party and which strive to present purely factual information. Comfort tools are communications from one party to another and depend more on conventions and norms than on predetermined formats.

Perhaps one of the best known comfort tools is the organizational chart. As any manager knows, this is the arrangement of boxes and lines which seeks to communicate the positions in an organization, their reporting relationships to each other, and their official lines of communication. Organizational charts are so familiar and comfortable that they show up in everything from grant proposals to lending materials to annual reports.

They're also usually wrong.

Here's why. Organizational charts are all about position, responsibility, and apparent power. In reality, they don't convey any of those things. Why? Because they are a function of relationships, and relationships can't get communicated neatly on paper. More important, the changes in nonprofit management are fast rendering the organizational chart downright quaint.

YOU CAN BLAME SCIENTIFIC MANAGEMENT

Today's organizational chart is a by-product of scientific management, which was the brainchild of Frederick Winslow Taylor, an early Industrial Age theorist who was the Peter Drucker of his day and whose theories about productivity are so widely accepted today that the man himself is virtually unknown. The bedrock implication of scientific management—as opposed to the decidedly nonscientific practices of late nineteenth century manufacturing—is that most of the job of management can be quantified, analyzed, and improved upon almost infinitely. And, in that quest, management's interests are inherently opposed to those of the workers.

Traditional organizational charts support this logic by describing organizations as a series of interconnected boxes arrayed in pyramid style. That it has survived this long is a testament to its simplicity and power.

The simple organizational chart in Figure 6 communicates many familiar messages. Overall, its theme is that people in this organization all have positions that exist in a familiar and understandable re-

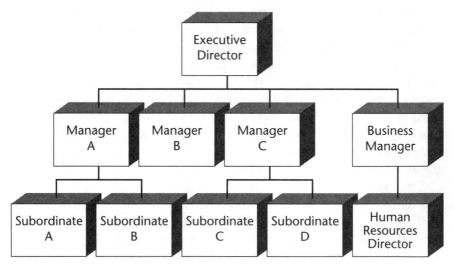

Figure 6. Typical Nonprofit, Inc.

lationship to each other. Ideas and information are expected to flow through established channels from the top down for directives, from the bottom up for corrections and feedback when solicited.

ONE SIZE DOESN'T FIT ALL

But there is a problem with traditional organizational charts as they apply to nonprofit organizations. The truth is that most nonprofit organizations—and for-profit service providers as well—have never fit comfortably into the traditional organizational chart. For one thing, most nonprofits have never been quite rich enough to afford all those levels of middle management (and, owing to the pervasiveness of the classic model, they've usually felt a bit inadequate about it).

For another, Taylor's management system was built for manufacturers. In economic terms, nonprofits are service providers, not product producers. It is arbitrary at best to suggest that middle managers in a nonprofit service provision environment are not providing every bit as much direct service—albeit not full-time—as the occupants of the very lowest boxes. So most of the underlying logic of managers being a distinct and even adversarial class with those below breaks down in nonprofit environments.

In short, the traditional organizational chart may have once worked well for machine shops and automakers, but it has always been a somewhat uneasy fit with the realities of nonprofit management. What really happens in most organizations is something completely different from the implied story of the traditional organizational chart. What happens most often has more to do with authority deriving from relationships than with authority deriving from positions on a chart.

Figure 7 attempts to explain the way nonprofit organizations usually work. We call it the New Organizational Chart, but it's probably more like an honest rendering of how things get done in the agency described in a traditional organizational chart.

In this chart the lines try to reflect communication channels rather than reporting channels (they could also reflect reporting relationships by using color or a different version of the chart). Also, the spheres of activity implicit in the traditional organizational chart have been replaced by clear lines of involvement, seen here as larger

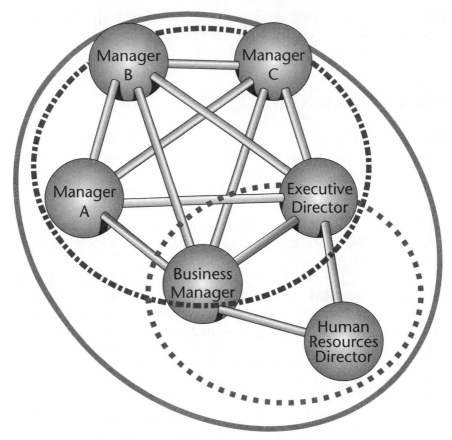

Figure 7.   New Organizational Chart

circles. Equally important, this chart explicitly acknowledges that there are overlapping areas of concern, which is something that most people in any organization recognize after about two days on the job but never quite know how to reconcile with the stated reality.

There are two such spheres of involvement in this simple example. One is related to services and programs and the other to fiscal and administrative. This is why the managers operate in the program sphere but have direct lines to the business manager in the financial and administrative sphere. Conversely, the executive director operates in both spheres, and in this organization is the only person to do so.

IT'S ABOUT RELATIONSHIPS

The largest underlying difference between traditional organizational charts and the new model, however, is that the new chart virtually abandons any focus on *position* in the agency and instead concentrates on *relationships*. In the traditional Industrial Age manufacturing company, knowing who occupied what position was important because it revealed something about what information they could be expected to know and about their authority to act on it.

In Information Age companies—and in nonprofits generally—information and its transfer are more important than authority. For example, the information contained in a client record usually has to be widely available within a nonprofit organization, and the authority to act on it tends to come from decisions made without regard to position but rather to relationship with the client. This is another illustration of why nonprofits have traditionally been a poor fit with traditional organizational charts.

In our hypothetical organization, the executive director has a relationship with all managers and operates in both spheres of activity. The human resources director, by contrast, functions largely with the executive director and the business manager and is effectively removed from anything happening in programs and services.

Another advantage of this style of charting is that it can be redrawn easily, reflecting changes in the sphere of activity in which individuals move, and showing more or fewer channels of communication with other positions. Finally, the chart itself, in spite of first impressions, is a fairly simple document. Programs can be added to a manager's scope simply by listing them in the appropriate circle. In fact, one could even argue that all managers could be represented by a single circle, thereby simplifying the document even further.

HERE COMES A GRANT REVIEWER (LOSE THE CHART)

Now back to reality. A grant proposal containing such a chart would probably be laughed off the boardroom table. Even a serious internal management document based on a chart like this might cause perplexed frowns and stifled giggles. The traditional organizational chart is so clear and simple for most people that an ambitious re-structuring is just not going to be acceptable.

Unfortunately, one must accept that old habits, not to mention old organizational structures, die hard. If this new rendering has any appeal to you, adapt it for yourself. Play with it, explore the possibilities, study its meaning. Share it with a few people and see how far it goes. All the while, be fully aware that this idea of a new organizational chart may be preposterous daydreaming.

Then again, not too long ago you could have said it was preposterous to have a computer on everyone's desk.

The Permanent
Labor Shortage

Veteran nonprofit managers feel shivers of fear the first time they see Help Wanted signs sprouting in fast food restaurants. Like the first snowflakes in fall, those innocuous signs inevitably signal the beginning of a long cold spell for nonprofit hiring. Those signs first started appearing in the mid-1990s in some areas of the country. As of this writing, most labor markets range from hot to white hot. Hiring good employees is fast becoming the overriding operational goal of many nonprofits in virtually all fields.

We've been through this before. There was another labor shortage in the mid-1980s. Unfortunately for Wall Street, but fortunately for nonprofit managers, that one ended when a recession began. Jobs in direct services that didn't look all that attractive a few years before suddenly looked to newly laid-off workers like a pretty good alternative.

But the current labor shortage is different. In fact, you might want to brace yourself. It looks like the labor shortage of the last few years is going to be permanent.

Why? Labor markets are cyclical creatures. What's in short supply in one era is oversupplied in the next. Why won't the same thing happen again?

WHY IT'S HAPPENING

The answer lies in a number of things that have changed. Taken together, their effect is unprecedented, and the impact is likely to be long-lived. Here are some of the reasons for the permanent labor shortage.

Start with the growth in the number of nonprofits. Beginning in the late 1980s, the number of nonprofit corporations operating in the United States increased by 50 percent. Imagine that rate of growth in your neighborhood, where ten years ago there were twenty houses and today there are thirty. Even if plenty of land is available, that kind of growth changes many things about the place where you live.

Along with growth in the numbers of nonprofits came an increase in employment. We shifted to a service-based economy long ago, so in the eight years ending in 1995 it was no surprise that the manufacturing sector suffered a net loss of employment. By contrast, governmental employment grew by a little under 2 percent, total for-profit employment grew by 3 percent, and nonprofits outstripped them both with a strong 3.5 percent growth in employment.

Now throw in the nature of the work. Direct service jobs in most nonprofit organizations—the positions that are the most numerous and see the most turnover—are increasingly low-skilled jobs. Managers and those with some form of professional certification are a very different class of worker. But the central economic fact is that most of the work does not need to be done by degreed or highly trained people.

Consequently, nonprofits tend to employ large numbers of young people. This is the labor force that is most adaptable, most likely to work for entry-level wages, and most likely to contract or expand depending on need.

This labor force (those in the 16- to 34-year-old range) peaked at about 9 percent of the total labor force in 1979–1980 and then plummeted, reaching a low of about 3 percent in 1998, a level that hadn't been seen since 1968. Not coincidentally, the peak years for this population coincided with the greatest previous growth spurt in the total number of nonprofits as governments began massively privatizing social services in the 1970s and early 1980s.

To this already potent stew add the fiscal stagnation of many nonprofit service providers in recent years as government funders initiated managed care programs or, more heavy-handedly, simply level-funded or cut back many services. A compensation pool that was never very rich became dangerously thin.

The final factor—undocumented but perhaps the most profound of all—is the death of the Peace Corps. Yes, the effort still exists, but the idealism of the 1960s Peace Corps volunteers was a strong cultural force that does not exist today. Many of today's nonprofit leaders have some sort of Peace Corps involvement in their past and still carry their own middle-aged version of that enthusiasm. Even more important, that 1960s idealism gave public service a seal of approval that made it socially okay to work in nonprofit agencies. There is no such powerfully sanctioning governmental body for public service in existence today.

The result is that the nonprofit workforce has effectively been positioned as a kind of mediating body that originally swelled to accommodate others sectors' lost employees but now is forced to give some of them back.

WHAT TO DO?

It has become a cliché to say that nonprofits must get better at retaining employees, but it is nonetheless true. The greater value in the platitude comes from analyzing it. What does it really mean to get better at retaining employees? It's a complicated undertaking, and there is no single thing that will increase agencies' retention abilities, but underneath it all the sentiment means that nonprofits must professionalize their human resource function.

Whereas executive directors in the 1970s and 1980s often worked hard to be able to afford a grantwriter, today's executives often put a human resource professional at the head of their wish list. Even if an HR person does nothing more than help the agency avoid common pitfalls, it can have a decided effect on employee retention rates.

Accepting the new realities of the labor market will also help. Many nonprofits have been so accustomed to a one-size-fits-all approach to benefits design that they forget the power of key benefits. For instance, the instinct to pay as little as possible toward health insurance benefits practically guarantees that the organization will be attractive only to young healthy singles for whom this is the best deal. But if the organization decides that its best employee prospects are older married adults, an appropriately designed health insurance policy may be more attractive than an equivalent amount in salary.

Nonprofits are already growing more innovative about tapping into new pools. Some are recruiting overseas, offering signing bonuses, and promising financial incentives to employees to refer friends. This will have to continue and get even more ingenious if organizations are to survive the labor crunch.

Producing efficiencies is an underappreciated source of dollars for staff raises. Many nonprofits are highly inefficient when it comes to ordinary things like using telecommunications to eliminate travel time and minimize financial management staff effort. The good news here is that just a 1 percent efficiency across the board, if applied to raising staff salaries, would produce an average 1.5 percent compensation increase (because that 1 percent only needs to be applied to the average 70 percent of the budget in personnel costs in an average agency).

Demographics may soon help, once again. We are in the beginning stages of the years when echo boomers—the baby boomers' children—will begin entering the work force in large numbers. The number of teenagers is expected to rise by 5 million by 2005. The sheer numbers are encouraging even if only a fraction choose to work in nonprofits.

As Yogi Berra said, predictions are hard to make, especially about the future. There is no way of knowing what environmental shift is bearing down upon us—McDonald's is experimenting with fully automated restaurants; will that expand or contract the entry-level labor pool? Still, it's difficult to see how the current labor crunch will ever completely go away. More than likely it will be with us—to one degree or another—for the next several years. Hot labor markets create a lot of heat.

It's 2010: Do You Know Who Your Executive Director Is?

Fresh out of a master's degree program, the new graduate was brimming with ideas and energy. Intrigued by this brand-new international volunteer program called the Peace Corps, he interviewed for a slot and was accepted. For the next two years—three if you count training time and the extra months he spent wrapping up the project—he immersed himself in a village irrigation project in a third world country. It was exhausting work, but he ended it with more energy and commitment to social change than ever before.

Back in this country, he was momentarily directionless. It was difficult to reorient himself to the increasingly tumultuous domestic scene of the mid-1960s. Needing money and a way to "plug in," he took a job as a house parent for another innovative program, a group home for mentally retarded adults. It too was exhausting work, but he loved it just as much.

After a year or two, he was asked to supervise a few other house parents. A few years later, he was in charge of a significant portion of the small organization's programs. Then the executive director unexpectedly resigned, and he stepped in to take her place.

Today, the agency is one of the largest of its kind in the region, and he is its respected, long-time leader. He has guided the organization through rapid growth and has secured the admiration and gratitude of the thousands of citizens he has served through a dizzying array of programs and services.

Personally, he is comfortable. His children are grown and have children of their own. He and his wife are enjoying their newfound time together. And every day when he goes to work, the thought crosses his mind: *I'm 60 years old. I don't want to do this much longer. I need to find a way out . . .*

This scenario is fiction. And yet it is true. The social activism of the 1960s and 1970s spawned a whole generation of nonprofit leaders who are now close to retirement. Many have been quite successful, but now they face a challenge unlike any they have faced before: ensuring continuity of leadership.

SUCCESSION PLANNING

In the for-profit world the conventional response to this dilemma is called *succession planning,* and it occurs with great frequency among organizations large and small. The aging CEO names a second-in-command with the explicit intention of turning over the firm within a few years; the daughters and sons of a successful small businessman decide among themselves who will continue the company's business and in what role. These scenarios are common in the business environment because those with an economic stake in an enterprise understand the importance of continuity to its success. But there is no counterpart in the nonprofit world.

Why not? Comparatively, the executive director job in a nonprofit corporation is potentially one of the most powerful positions in American society. Without the inherent authority of ownership, which confers authority via capital, a nonprofit manager must achieve authority through a mixture of position, personality, values, and ideas. When all of those elements are aligned, they can produce enormous power for a single individual. In fact, it is an instinctive grasp of this possibility that attracts many people, like our mythical Peace Corps volunteer, to this field. The fact that they are often people of goodwill and solid ethical standards is heartening but in organizational terms only a bonus.

The positive side is that communities benefit tremendously from these entrepreneurial nonprofit executives. Over time they create opportunity for their organization's consumers, board members, staff, and the wider society. The downside is that they are the glue that makes it all work. Take away that glue and the organization suffers a lapse.

Sociologists call this *charismatic leadership,* and it is why many of today's visionary nonprofits may face trouble ahead. The strength and success of the entire organization depends so heavily on a single, talented individual that it has no real systems in place, and current momentum cannot easily be transferred to another person. It is important to understand that "charismatic" in this sense implies no judgment about success; it is just a descriptive term for how the organization operates. Even mediocre agencies can be said to use a charismatic leadership style.

WHAT TO DO?

As with so many management ills, the first step in dealing with the problem of succession planning is to recognize its existence. No one likes to admit his or her own mortality—and in the next ten years the current generation of age-denying, activist baby boomers will probably be the worst of all—but the fact remains that the mission of a nonprofit is jeopardized if its leadership cannot be sustained.

Tip: Is Your Agency Risking a Lapse in Leadership?

What would happen to your organization tomorrow if a sudden meteorite shower were to decimate your executive director's bedroom tonight? Here is a rough and admittedly imprecise (but useful) guide to an answer. Look at the salaries of your top five executives listed on your organization's IRS form 990. Look at the chief executive's salary and then find the next highest paid person in the organization. If that person is a senior manager arguably comparable to the CEO such as an assistant director, chief financial person, or chief program manager, breathe a bit easier. Next, look at the difference between the two salaries. If there is a spread of less than 20 percent, breathe even easier. Except in cases of extraordinary personal loyalty, senior managers' salaries tend to be a function of the local labor market. If the CEO believes that his or her deputies are worth almost as much as he or she is, he is probably right. If, on the other hand, the CEO believes his or her deputies are not worth nearly as much, he is almost certainly right—and the organization may have a difficult time finding a successor from within.

The next step is for the board of directors to get a clear idea of the organization's strategic position for the foreseeable future. To categorize it roughly, the desired strategic position will require either that the organization maintain what it currently has or achieve something different.

With a good, widely shared understanding of the nonprofit's strategic future, the board must then inventory existing management talent. Are the skills and knowledge required for the future position already in place? If not, can they be developed? Just as attaining a strategic position in a few years may necessitate acquiring competencies not currently in house (such as development or program specialists), the task of planning leadership succession may necessitate bringing on managers with complementary leadership potential.

To develop future leaders, give them leadership practice. Rarely will any organization officially and formally designate a given individual as a future CEO, but there can be a general consensus among board members as to who it might be. One mental health center assigned a senior manager to be in charge of the agency's application for professional accreditation. The two-year project was wildly successful, thereby marking her as a potential successor to the present executive director in virtually all board members' minds.

Don't rule out the possibility of merging with another organization as a solution to the leadership succession problem. Many people in the field have noted the role of government funding cutbacks and managed care in causing nonprofits to think about mergers, but in our experience leadership succession is at least as important.

Leadership succession is not the most pressing topic on most organizations' agenda. But, at least periodically, maybe it should be.

Why Mergers Fail, and What To Do About It

As more nonprofit organizations are choosing mergers as a strategic direction, we are learning more about what works and what doesn't work. While many nonprofits have successfully merged their operations, other nonprofits have failed at the attempt. Early research, such as that done by David LaPiana, suggests that predictable roadblocks like picking the new executive director and blending different cultures are often the culprits for failed mergers. More research is needed to expand our knowledge of these areas, and to detail the reasons why these topics become "dealbreakers."

But for practitioners—including executive directors, board members, and even funding source representatives—the truth is simple and eloquent. Mergers fail because people want them to fail.

THE TWO BIG E'S

Every merger encounters resistance. A merger is a big idea, and big ideas are never accepted unanimously by any group of thinking individuals. The resistance can take many different forms, be active or passive, and come from a virtually unlimited number of people and institutions. The important thing is not whether the merger encounters resistance but how it is handled. And the key to handling resistance is understanding it.

Most resistance to a merger proposal will derive from what we call the two Big E's: ego and economics. These two big E's are large indeed, and require a concise response.

The idea of economics in this context is probably self-evident— fears of job loss and salary or benefit reductions are natural companions of the merger process. These must be dealt with rationally, honestly, and openly. Unfortunately, the media muddies the waters here. Wall Street's message to for-profit companies contemplating a merger is often some variation on "go ahead—but make sure we get something out of it." Usually what Wall Street wants is a bump up in the stock price, and the quickest way to get that is to slice jobs. Media outlets hungrily converge on such a story for its obvious human interest, which is why the term *merger* has come to be synonymous with *job loss* for anyone who regularly reads the morning paper or watches the evening news. The stakes couldn't be more different for nonprofits.

Ego as a term is normally associated with individuals, and that form of ego is absolutely a factor in resistance to a merger. The first and largest source of ego-based resistance is likely to be the executive director who doesn't want to have to send out Christmas cards announcing that he has just been demoted to assistant executive director. Close behind is the board president who "doesn't want to be known as the last president of this agency." Other executives also have economic reasons for resistance, in that they may fear job loss.

Another type of ego at work here is a more group-oriented phenomenon. Most commonly it gets expressed as pride in a group such as a department or even the whole organization. It can also be expressed as a strong preference for a certain management style or an ideology, concern for the community, the vague assertion that "their services aren't as good as ours," or even an impatience to "get this process going." Whatever the exact expression of this kind of ego, it can be a powerful source of resistance (note that, in the example of impatience, it may paradoxically lead to resistance by creating it on the part of the other organization).

Ego-based resistance is best dealt with symbolically. The smaller organization in a merger may feel less like it is being taken over if a majority of meetings are held in its office, or if the new entity adopts its name. The time and place of the planning committee meetings may be symbolically important ("Our board always meets on the third Tuesday of every month."). The use of names in the new entity is of utmost importance, and so on. Like it or not, much of the richness of the merger dialog occurs on a symbolic level. Participants who are not aware of this, or who operate as though it doesn't exist, run the very real risk of slowing the merger and possibly scuttling it altogether.

BOARD MEMBERS' RESISTANCE

For board members, ego often means the institutional identification that they feel, although it can also refer to the raw personal ego stake that some develop. Several things make board member resistance easier to deal with than almost any other kind. In general, one will not find a more sincere group of well-meaning people than board members of nonprofit organizations. Whatever their personal styles or ideologies, they usually want to do the right thing for the people and the community they serve. Most are keenly aware of their fiduciary responsibility.

Boards usually need to be sold on the idea of a merger. And why not? They are the ones with the legally constituted authority, and they have every right to consider such a major decision carefully. Someone needs to present the facts to them. They may need and want guidance in interpreting those facts, and they will certainly want to debate the idea. If the initiators of the merger—usually management or perhaps funding sources—have made their own decision on the merits of the case, the board can reasonably be expected to come to the same conclusion. If they don't do so after a careful, nonpressured review, then the proposal may deserve at least a rethinking if not tabling.

MIDDLE MANAGERS' RESISTANCE

In mergers as in life, there is no group more conservative than the newly arrived. Those who have just recently made it according to the old rules understandably don't want them changed. This is the ego aspect of manager resistance. The economic motivations come from the fact that people who have been smart enough to earn a management job are smart enough to figure out that if jobs are to be cut it is theirs that are the most vulnerable.

The ticklish part about manager resistance is that it is rarely explicit. Many times there is little or no verbal resistance at all, perhaps because reluctant managers realize that it would be foolish to directly oppose the merger process once it gets started. Instead, the ostensible verbal agreement is subverted by inaction, delay, and diversion. After a while, resistant managers usually stamp themselves as such by the fact that they never actually accomplish the tasks they are assigned during the merger process. Resistant managers are essentially gambling that they will be able to stop the merger, because they are less likely to have a meaningful role in the entity whose creation they opposed.

UNIONS' RESISTANCE

Unions are potentially rich sources of resistance because they have both ego and economic reasons for opposing collaboration. Many nonprofit managers are fundamentally sympathetic to labor unions even if they are angered or disillusioned by some of the day-to-day realities of a collective bargaining environment. This leads to a quiet ambivalence on the manager's part, which can play itself out in erratic behavior in union relation matters. It can also lead to a downright hostile environment if both senior management and union personnel let personal feelings get in the way of business dealings.

Again, the preferred strategy is straightforward, merits-of-the-case negotiation. A sensitively handled merger process may actually improve the overall level of union–management relations.

FUNDING SOURCES MAY ALSO RESIST

Government funding sources act as a proxy for the open market in many nonprofit arenas and, consequently, are instrumental in forcing the conditions in which mergers are advisable. For this reason, higher levels of government agencies usually do not resist a merger. And anyway, it is legally and politically wise for them to maintain official neutrality. They are rarely in a position to demand or block a merger, and a statement of neutrality is as close to approval as one is likely to get.

The story is different deeper in the bureaucracy, however. Field office managers, in-house attorneys, and even financial analysts sometimes feel threatened by the prospect of a merger if they see their job as one of maintaining command and control authority over the groups they fund. Strategic mergers consolidate power in the private nonprofit sector, and in return for giving up a measure of short-term control the government official gains the ability to profoundly shape and influence the future. This should be an appropriate trade-off for governmental work in the new information age, but not all officials see it that way. Happily, these guerrilla control efforts usually extinguish themselves although it may require a little careful exposing of them to hasten the process.

Properly handled, the idea of a merger can be a unifying and broadening experience for many people in an organization. Still, there will always be resistance to it. How that resistance is understood and handled will go a long way toward determining whether the merger is a success or not.

Boys and Girls

S omeone has to say it.
There are boy agencies. And there are girl agencies.
The differences between them are real, predictable, and sometimes dramatic. Ignoring the differences is risky. Understanding them and working with them can help lead to success.

RELATIONSHIPS THE KEY

In a word, the source of the major differences is the way managers think about power. Over time, the personality and style of the chief executive officer indelibly stamps the agency he or she leads. Most of the time the elements of that stamp are subtle. But taken as a whole they paint a distinct portrait of a management style. It is to the broad outlines of that style, as it relates to power, that we are referring when we speak of boy agencies and girl agencies.

Everyone knows how important it is for those inside an organization to understand the tendencies of its leadership. For reasons ranging from professional survival to organizational effectiveness, staff and board members of a nonprofit need to feel that leadership will act somewhat predictably. But mergers, strategic alliances, and collaboration among agencies will be the story of the early twenty-first century for most nonprofits and this means that agencies have to learn how to work with outsiders far more than ever before.

As a result, the organizational "personality" of a nonprofit will get more attention. Those who intuitively understand this central fact or who have been closely connected with more than one nonprofit will grasp the nature of organizational personalities immediately. Those with more limited experience may not sense how powerful the concept can be. Dealing with the implications of different management styles is much easier if one can recognize the existence and origins of those styles.

This is not about differentiating agencies solely on the basis of the gender of the chief executive officer. Nor is it about statistical predictability. Beyond a certain size most nonprofits exhibit tendencies of both types of agencies. But the more an organization displays a distinctive style the more likely it will be on one side or the other of this fundamental split. The following observations are most valid and useful with small- to medium-size nonprofits, or just about any large institution that has had consistent leadership over a long period of time. Large entities such as hospitals and universities are more complex and more difficult to characterize accurately based on a single manager's style. They are simply harder for a single individual or small group of people to influence.

Here are a few of the more interesting and significant ways that these agencies differ.

Source of power. In male-oriented agencies power tends to come from position. In female-oriented agencies power tends to come from relationships. Male agencies always have an updated organizational chart available. Many actually believe it. Power is perceived as originating at the top and being distributed down through the organization. In female agencies, on the other hand, the chief executive officer is more likely to be perceived—usually by herself as well as others—as being at the center of an intricate web of connections.

There are several consequences to this pattern. One is that male CEO's tend to be more comfortable in production-oriented settings—hospitals, mental health clinics, vocational training services, etc. Male agencies may delegate sparingly since giving up power is seen as threatening position. Relationship-based management is better suited to situations where influence, persuasion, and personal contact are critical. This is why women will find it easier to operate in some of the strategic alliances currently developing in health care and social services.

If power comes from position in a male agency, it is exercised against a backdrop of rules and regulations. Just as an organizational chart makes relationships easier to deal with by making them clearer and more precisely defined, rules and regulations (from out-

> ## The Merger That Didn't Work
>
> One was an old boys' agency.
> The other was an old girls' agency.
> "Let's get this merger done right away," said the boys' group.
> "Let's talk about it," said the girls' group.
> "Okay, but we don't want to waste time."
> "You're not listening to us."

siders such as the government, or from insiders) define the bounds of behavior within those relationships. To exaggerate only slightly, male agencies communicate behavioral expectations through memos, female agencies through notes in paychecks.

Use of technology. Male agencies are quicker to adopt new technologies. This follows naturally from the emphasis on production. Technology at its best is essentially a productivity tool. However, there is probably a subtle dynamic at work that governs the comfort with which technology is embraced.

For-profit businesses historically adopt technology because they see a continuum of resources with human labor on one end and machines on the other. The further along this continuum they can move toward machines, the more profitable their business. It is the starkest of zero-sum games: more machines, fewer people.

With their institutional interest in production and a need to de-emphasize personal relationships, male agencies will find comfort in technological solutions. Female agencies may adopt it for the most obvious areas, such as financial systems, but otherwise they are less interested. Why make a change which threatens their preferred means for getting things done?

Types of related parties. *Related parties* in a nonprofit corporation are situations where a person in a position of power and influence, such as a manager or member of the board of directors, stands to benefit personally from some aspect of the corporation's business. For example, if a museum board member who is also an architect designs the museum's new wing, it is a related party relationship. Related party transactions may or may not be inappropriate, but they should always be disclosed to outsiders.

Male agencies and female agencies enter into related party transactions differently. Male agencies tend to do it via contract, in keeping with their preference for rules and regulations. From the previous example, the board member/architect's business relationship with the agency will be as a contracted entity. Female agencies, on the other hand, tend to enter into related party transactions that are more personal in nature. For example, the executive director's husband may hold a part-time position with the organization, or a senior manager's son might be a program director. You get the idea. There are differences between nonprofits, and boy/girl is one of the biggest. Keep this idea in mind the next time you can't figure out why the agency across town does things the way it does.

Managing Different Kinds of Diversity

We can be forgiven if we routinely assume that diversity is a matter of ethnicity and heritage. These are such fundamental aspects of our political, economic, and interpersonal dialogs that they get a lot of deserved attention. But many other kinds of diversity frequently play a more crucial role in the day-to-day management of nonprofit organizations. As stated earlier, gender differences are one of the most unrecognized sources of this diversity. Nonprofits that are growing and those that work closely with other nonprofits have to find ways of dealing with the diversity that derives from these other, less obvious sources. Here are some more, along with some suggestions for managing them.

ATTITUDE TOWARD RISK

To get one kind of indicator of organizational philosophy about risk, go to line 64 in the balance sheet section of the IRS Nonprofit Tax Form 990. This is the amount of long-term debt—mortgages and the like—that the organization carries. Other than in the case of new or very small agencies, a zero in this line probably means the nonprofit is risk averse.

One of the most powerful wellsprings of diversity in nonprofits is organizational attitude toward risk. On the surface, it may seem that an aversion to risk is inherent to nonprofits. Board members are legally regarded as fiduciaries of the nonprofit organizations they serve. As such, and without a profit motive, there is little incentive for board members to expose themselves to the massive risks sometimes involved in developing new services or innovating. In truth, the mission of a nonprofit is not to avoid risk but to accomplish something for the public good.

Because the perception of risk tends to be greatest in the absence of information, risk-averse nonprofits tend to be isolated and less knowledgeable about their environments. This leads to management by mythology and a siege mentality. Safe decisions are prized, and often the logical outcome is a tendency to avoid risk by avoiding decisions.

This attitude tends to spill over into more mundane matters as well. Hiring decisions are made with an implicit desire to maintain the status quo, which is to say a low-risk, low-conflict atmosphere. Paralysis eventually sets in until something jars the organization onto a different track.

The antidote to the overly risk-averse culture is a combination of values and education. Often their desired values are similar to those of nonprofits more comfortable with risk. The difference lies in how one gets there. For two agencies trying to work together, it can be enormously helpful to realize that they share the same values and beliefs, and that their major difference lies in how they embody those values.

For those managing diverse attitudes toward risk within an agency, education can be a big help. For instance, board members unwilling to consider allowing the agency to take out a mortgage may need to learn that profitability is the only other realistic source of expansion funding, and that a refusal to borrow may be equivalent to reduced effectiveness. Or, they may simply need to understand the limited nature of their own liability.

ENTREPRENEURSHIP VERSUS STEWARDSHIP

The two mental health centers seeking to merge could not have been more different. One was an older, well-established though declining agency whose culture emphasized clinical credentials from respectable graduate programs, traditional services, and regulatory compliance. The other was a fast-paced, innovative, and rapidly

*growing center whose services were beginning to expand the limits of
what it meant to provide mental health care.*

Closely related to philosophies of risk, an increasing number of
nonprofits are developing an entrepreneurial spirit. Unlike attitudes
toward risk, however, entrepreneurial change is likely to cause far
more conflict within an organization than between organizations.
What causes internal conflict is usually the unique demands of entrepreneurial activity. The fast-paced nature of most entrepreneurial
leadership tends to make working environments unpredictable and
seemingly unstable, conditions under which many people don't like
working.

In most instances in a nonprofit, there is—initially, at least—only
one or two true entrepreneurs, and one of them is usually the executive director. Even in organizations noted for their innovation and
fast pace, there are often only one or a handful of entrepreneurial
types. Partly this is because it's hard to live with a large number of
round-the-clock entrepreneurs, so an agency culture just won't accept it. It's also due to the fact that nonprofit laws and regulations
rightfully discourage fortune-seeking, so the nonprofit entrepreneur is still a relative rarity.

Accommodating an entrepreneurial executive director often requires a buffer, a trusted individual or group of senior managers
who can act as intermediaries to support the executive director
while making sure that the staff gets the work done. Many staff
members just want a calm, reliable working atmosphere with the
benefits of entrepreneurial action as long as they don't have to experience much of it firsthand. Who can blame them?

When an innovative agency tries to get together with a more traditional one, they both need to manage the diversity. Finding and
stressing common values can help, as does leadership. In the previous example, a pivotal board member from the older agency re-
alized that eventually there would only be room in their region for
one mental health center and he strongly supported the merger. For
her part, the executive director was able to harness her entrepreneurial energies long enough to craft a merger agreement with
which both cultures could agree. The integration period stretched
over several years and involved a lot of internal discussion and
recommitment to the mission, but today the organization is
stronger for it.

GEOGRAPHY

The elder service case manager scowled as she signed out for the day. "I'll be out at that training session tomorrow," she told a colleague standing nearby.

"What's the matter? I thought you wanted to go to that training session."

"I do. I just don't want to go over the bridge to get to it," she said, referring to the structure that connected her island-like resort area to the rest of the state. "I hate going over the bridge."

Her colleague laughed lightly at the joke, but the case manager slapped down the pencil and walked out the door. She wasn't joking.

Geography is one of the most natural and enduring elements to divide people and agencies. The existence of bridges, lakes, railroad tracks, mountains, islands, and long stretches of highway between agencies provide both real and symbolic barriers preventing communication and a sense of community among agencies. True, much of the division is basically socioeconomic, but physical geographic features crystallize the differences and they are among the hardest to overcome.

Nonprofit agencies can't remove the bridges and mountains that stand between them and their peers, but they can change the way they manage the organizational impact of those geographic barriers. The formation of management companies, administrative services organizations, and large, multidivision agencies are good ways of incorporating the differences rather than trying to fight them. Again, developing and maintaining a clear mission and shared values can help diminish the negatives of geographic diversity. Agency-wide projects (such as accreditation or major expansion), as well as common training programs and low barriers to personnel interchanges, can also help.

SERVICE MODELS

The disability services agency owned a large building in which they ran a sheltered workshop for several dozen clients. Their potential merger partner was a residential services provider with two dozen sites and a small, supported employment program. At the first meet-

ing of the merger committee, the issue of sheltered workshops grew into a heated debate. "Sheltered workshops exploit clients and can't possibly be helpful settings," said the residential provider. "We provide an opportunity to work for clients who otherwise wouldn't have such an opportunity," countered the workshop leaders. The merger never occurred.

Diversity based on models of service is one of the most intractable kinds of diversity and one of the hardest to manage because it is rooted in differing values. Methadone maintenance for drug addicts, aversive therapy for autistic children, and sheltered workshops for disabled people are just three controversial models of service.

Ideology is at the heart of these differences, so it is practicality that must overcome them. As with some of the other types of diversity described above, it may help to have a large enough service system to incorporate programs using these models. Full continuums of service should be able to offer controversial niche services without compromising their overall values, particularly if the service has external support. The advantage of a pragmatic, nonideological approach is that it makes external funders the arbiters of program models. If a funding source decides that it wants to pay for a controversial service, it will be in the system's interests to provide it. If not, the service will eventually fade anyway.

Diversity comes in many different packages. The most common and hard to recognize kinds are the ones that show up in daily operations and have misleading labels. Fortunately, it's possible to manage these less obvious kinds of diversity. It just takes being open to new ways of doing things.

Why Board Members Wake Up at 3:00 A.M.

The popular and successful corporate executive has reached that certain point in his career. His record of accomplishment speaks for itself, and a few doors are beginning to open even before he knocks. He's been thinking about giving something back to the community, so he's more than receptive when he's invited to join the board of directors of that nonprofit organization.

But he has a few questions first. Question number one is "How much time will it take?" and question number two is "Will I have to do any fundraising?" The board member or corporate officer extending the invitation is ready for these questions and answers reassuringly. No boilerplate answers here; they've done their homework, and they already know exactly how to incorporate his needs and abilities into the existing board of directors.

He relaxes a moment, contemplating the satisfaction of community service. It's only later that night—at three o'clock in the morning, to be precise—that he wakes up with a dagger of fear in his heart: "Am I going to get sued?"

This is a perfectly legitimate question, and there is anecdotal evidence that nonprofits have been the object of unwanted litigious attention in recent years (for example, wrongful discharge, particularly of an executive director, is an especially popular grounds for a suit). What the rookie board member may not know is that nonprofits in many states enjoy a measure of protection from lawsuits. English common law, upon which a great deal of our laws are based, tacitly provided protection from lawsuits for quasi-public agents that we would today call nonprofit organizations. Some states have explicitly provided nonprofits protections based on these antecedents. And the obvious poverty of many nonprofits discourages potential plaintiffs seeking deep pockets.

But the real misunderstanding about legal liability lies in the way that we think about lawsuits in this sector. High visibility lawsuits against for-profit boards of directors as a group are a relatively new phenomenon in this country, but they have subtly shaped our assumptions about how nonprofit boards are at risk. Transferring the proprietary corporation experience to the nonprofit sector is terribly misleading for many reasons. For one, many suits originate from stockholders angered by the way the board handled a buyout, acquisition, or similar venture. While nonprofit corporations often have active members too, by definition they cannot be stockholders and so there isn't the same potential economic tension between the two groups. Also, on a very practical level, many legal challenges to for-profit boards derive from product liability and the vast majority of nonprofit organizations are service providers, sometimes in fields where malpractice is virtually impossible to define. Not to be overlooked is the fact that the boards of major corporations typically include individuals who would be extremely deep-pocketed defendants in their own right. When the average nonprofit board includes the merely affluent serving with the potential protection of their state's laws, the economics of a suit are profoundly different.

One group that hasn't missed the nature of nonprofit board liability is the insurance companies and agencies that serve the nonprofit market. During the liability insurance crisis of the mid-1980s the directors and officers (D & O) insurance market collapsed, going from a total of over fifty companies writing the coverage to fewer than ten. Nonprofit organizations desiring the coverage—not to mention their proprietary counterparts—had to scramble for replacement carriers, and at one point there were only a few programs actively offering new D & O policies to nonprofit organizations. Today the pendulum has swung back in the other direction, with many insurance agencies and companies recognizing the potentially lucrative nonprofit market for both D & O and other types of coverage as well.

So, that respected local executive considering serving on a nonprofit board who worries about his personal risk is doing something perfectly understandable, even if the evidence doesn't support it. He simply needs to understand that being successful in business means routinely taking a long series of risks. Being on the board of directors of a nonprofit public charity is near the bottom of the list.

Why "Corporate" Board Members May Fail

If nonprofits were professional football teams, the Heisman Trophy winner hungrily sought by all would be the "corporate" board member. The local equivalent of the Heisman is an executive from a major corporation who is willing to join the board in a volunteer capacity to lend his or her expertise. These sought-after individuals typically come with ready-made, certifiable expertise and the credibility of being part of a nationally recognized organization. In short, they are expected to be virtually guaranteed winners. And, by the way, they may be able to toss a few of those big corporate bucks in the agency's direction.

Most of the time these board members are a credit to their employer and an asset to the nonprofit. But often the executive director—quietly, for to say it out loud would be highly impolitic and ungracious—is disappointed. Why? The answer is complex but surprisingly predictable, and is largely rooted in unrealistic expectations and a misreading of corporate culture.

MONEY NOT FORTHCOMING

Start with the money. Most executive directors sincerely want the benefit of the corporate executive's knowledge but may also harbor the unspoken hope that the individual might eventually prove to be a good fundraiser. This often doesn't work, for two reasons. First, the skills needed to be a successful executive are not necessarily the same as those needed to be good fundraiser. Second, corporate

119

America is restructuring, and philanthropic decisions are often made in another city. This disempowers executives from everywhere but the corporate office when it comes to setting the fundraising agenda.

"JUST ANOTHER BOARD MEMBER"

Beyond the money question, the disappointment tends to take the form of an assessment of the executive as "just another board member." Again, this tends to be a quiet evaluation, perhaps not even shared with anyone else. The implication is that the executive was expected to be a standout, a true board leader.

Corporate executives are well qualified in their fields and usually achieve their positions after a lifelong screening process that begins well before they even join the company. As a result, few such individuals will be total failures, and in the end most are said to have done a creditable job. So what accounts for the subtle discrepancy between promise and performance?

FOUR REASONS

There are at least four reasons why corporate board members may not deliver on the promise that the nonprofit executive—and even other board members—feel they offer.

The first and most fundamental reason is the differing nature of the executive director's work requirements as compared with that of the typical board member from the corporate world. What many executive directors fail to recognize is the difference between being an executive, even in a nonprofit setting, and being a manager. The nonprofit executive director has ultimate responsibility for helping set and implement the agency's strategic direction, and so does the CEO in a for-profit company.

The real role of the executive, however, is to help his or her organization cope with change. Especially in a small- or medium-size nonprofit, the executive director is the only person situated to have both the broad-based information and the resources necessary to perform this job. Whether it happens or not is immaterial; structurally, that is the executive director's role. Managers, on the other hand, spend most of their time helping their organizations cope with complexity.

Though the person's job title may include the word "executive," the Fortune 1000 employee on the board may, in fact, be used to acting far more often as a manager than as an executive. He or she may have a largely technical job (such as information systems or finance) which is in many ways the complete opposite of an executive's role. They may deal with very different things on a day-to-day basis. For example, they may not even be accustomed to seeing monthly confidential corporate financial data. They may be uncomfortable making political decisions or accepting the degree of risk that any service provider must face.

Even if they act as a true executive in their job, their scope is likely to be limited. Worse, they may not even be aware of the difference. The result is that they may actually prefer to work in a more narrowly defined area without knowing it themselves. The executive director sees this as a lack of support, but it is really a preference for working in their proven comfort zone.

A second reason for disappointing results from corporate board members is their frequent lack of detailed knowledge about the field in which the nonprofit is active. This situation is virtually guaranteed by the structure of nonprofit boards. Volunteer board members cannot reasonably be expected to know a lot about their agency's field unless they are employed in it themselves—and if they were, they probably wouldn't be on the board. Again, the board member is forced to operate out of his or her comfort zone, and the result can be a letdown for hopeful executive directors.

The third reason why board members from corporate America may not live up to some expectations is simply because it is difficult to be a leader in two different fields simultaneously. Though this relates to the previous point in a narrow sense, it really has more to do with emotional commitment. One of the things that makes many executives successful in business is a large commitment of their personal psychological energy. This takes time, and rarely does an individual have the interest, the ability, and the time to be a true leader (as opposed to a figurehead) in both business and a nonprofit board.

Finally, service on a nonprofit board can be an intimidating experience (yes, really). To the typical corporate mind the lingo is different, the culture is strange, and the norms and values are hard to grasp. The natural reaction in this situation, especially in a volunteer setting, is to be less than confident about one's judgment and to defer to others whose assessment seems more reliable—such as the executive director. This is what leads to the phenomenon a colleague of mine refers to as board members "checking their business acumen at the door."

A REASSURING EXPERIENCE

Were they to read it differently, nonprofit executives might find this type of experience to be oddly reassuring. Volunteers from corporate America are not necessarily any better at managing than their nonprofit counterparts, they just get more recognition for it. Competence in the messy business known as leadership never springs from the tax code. The appearance of success as an executive often has more to do with the business environment than with the efforts of the individual.

Most of the problems described above stem from misperceptions and unrealistic expectations on the part of nonprofit executives and other board members. The first key to avoiding the problem is to be quite clear about corporate board members' personal skills and abilities. Seek individuals for the value they bring as individuals, not for the label they happen to carry. Most nonprofits are essentially small businesses, and success in a small business is usually achieved differently from the way success is achieved in a Fortune 1000 company.

Clearly assessing the skills and abilities desired in a board member may also lead in a different direction. Often our clients' most trusted board member for business advice is not a corporate executive but rather a local small business person who has confronted many of the same daily challenges as the agency faces.

It also helps to communicate expectations and hopes early in the relationship. The kind of corporate board member that many executive directors seek is as much a coach as anything else, and so it invariably comes down to a matter of personal chemistry. Even if the personal chemistry isn't there, a bona fide successful corporate type may be able to offer tips and techniques in his or her area of expertise. It's just not fair to expect them to walk across water to do it.

The Structure of National Boards of Directors

The national association's executive staff identifies a management goal and enlists local affiliates to help meet it. They work together to identify the problem and devise a plan of action. It is a strategy that everyone can live with, and perhaps it is even one in which the people who worked on it are proud. Yet at the next meeting of the association's board of directors, the proposal is voted down. Or tabled. Or met with disinterest. The national staff are left frustrated, the affiliates are puzzled and vow not to work so hard the next time, and everyone wonders why it happened.

IT'S THE STRUCTURE

The explanation for this common scenario lies in the nature of a national nonprofit association's board of directors. In this situation there are three distinct sets of institutional interests: the board, the national staff, and the affiliates' staff. In many cases the interests of the latter two parties is similar. The interests of the national board of directors, however, is a toss-up. Depending on the national board's composition, they may lean toward the other two parties' interpretation of things or they may go in an entirely different direction. Or they may be severely split and make no decisions at all.

To understand why this is so requires a bit of investigation into the nature of nonprofit boards as they operate on the national level.

For the typical community-based nonprofit the matter of board composition is well understood and even follows a recipe. You look for a few good businesspeople, a political type or two, some civic-minded leaders, and perhaps some kind of consumer representative. Sprinkle in an accountant, an attorney, a religious leader, and some wildcard members and you have a typical board.

One of the necessary structural weaknesses of nonprofit boards is that the directors generally can have no financial interest in the organization. This means that they must draw their rationale for serving from other sources such as a sense of civic or social responsibility or a desire for visibility in their community.

A corollary point is that if their nonprofit ever gets into trouble or makes some sort of misstep, members of the board of directors have a good chance of hearing about it from others in the community. There is a sense of connectedness and accountability to the local community.

What all this adds up to is a tenuous connection between board member and nonprofit reinforced largely through social relationships and identification with local areas. In large part, it works reasonably well. When it doesn't, the nonprofit's management can usually compensate.

LOCAL STRUCTURE, NATIONAL STAGE

Most of the national associations we speak of here are those that go beyond being a simple trade association. They offer other ways to unite their membership such as a national "brand" name or a defined program of services in return for membership. In these cases it is literally true that the national board of directors is a custodian of that brand and of the whole system. And on a national scale the relationships and mechanisms that work well locally are often hard to duplicate.

The reason is that national board members in such organizations are often chosen in precisely the same way that local board members are chosen, except that they tend to have some element of a national identity. So the local nonprofit's equivalent of the local business person is a Fortune 1000 executive, the consumer representative is from a national advocacy group, and so on. Alternatively, the national board may be composed of people from local affiliates' boards.

The problem with either method is that there is a fundamental gap between the typical executive director and his or her board members. Most nonprofit board members are not intimately familiar with their agency's industry and are often uninformed or intimidated about nonprofit management matters in general. Consequently, the national association's board of directors tends to reproduce this disconnectedness. What the outsider sees is inexplicable strategic lapses.

TWO REMEDIES

The easiest, although most unlikely, remedy is for national board members to recognize that there is a huge distance between their national role and the local interests of affiliates. When a role on a national board offers the chance to hear directly from leading thinkers in the field and to associate with interesting people in nice locations, it's hard to remember that the local affiliates' most pressing needs might be more oriented to fixing the leak in the record area ceiling.

The most powerful remedy is representation on governing boards. This can be controversial for a variety of reasons, but the credibility it offers and the goodwill it creates are essential to making the national/affiliate relationship work. Some may fear that including the affiliates' voice in governance matters may demean the organization (making it a "mere trade association") or create a conflict of interest for those board members, but neither is likely. Accomplishing common goals is easier when the voice of those at street level is empowered.

Why Small Is Beautiful for Boards of Directors

Nonprofit boards of directors represent the single largest potential force for forward-looking change in the organization, which is to say that they can also be the most regressive players too. The unspoken assessment of most nonprofit managers is that most boards fall in the latter category. There are various reasons for this situation, and many of these reasons are, unhappily, built into the nature of nonprofit corporations themselves.

One cause of board regressiveness that can be avoided, however, is the size of the board itself. In some circles, it is acceptable to build a board of directors larger than the cast of a Hollywood epic. The justifications for doing so range from a desire to spread widely the honor of membership (and its attendant possibilities for donations) to a peculiar notion of the board as a vehicle for communication. Often the board simply grows in size not from conscious choices but through inattention or as the easiest way to resolve one sticky issue or another.

Overgrowth like this creates a thoroughly hapless governing body. The payoff for the chief executive using this Machiavellian style is that he or she has unchallenged power. But, ultimately, this is a short-term gain, since it leaves the organization ill-equipped to deal with a major threat to its existence from the outside. The second advantage of smaller boards is that they provide fewer trees for board members to hide behind. As any graduate of an overenrolled public school knows, it is relatively easy to disappear into the middle of a large class without a trace. Some of us survived high school physics using this technique, but it is a poor way to build non-profit leadership. Smaller boards are the best way to ensure that everyone carries his or her own load.

Small boards also mean a more workable leadership structure. The real problem with large boards is that they allow for the possibility of too many leaders for the size of the job (see The Natural Laws of Task Forces in the next chapter). Finally, smaller boards are more apt to be focused on their job, which is to help the organization cope with change. Larger groups invite posturing and inattentiveness and, in an insidious way, their sheer size can make them come across as a shadow staff.

How small is small? Generally, boards of directors should fall somewhere in the seven to thirteen member range. One can make the total a bit higher to make room for must-have token board members such as key politicians, but even here one must consider the true effectiveness of such figureheads. Often the only thing that really gets accomplished is that the public figure feels guilty about not returning phone calls from the group—which of course may have been the reason he or she was placed on the board in the first place.

The best way to get a properly sized board of directors is not to let it get too large in the first place. Of course, the majority of boards in this situation are already operational, so the question becomes how one goes about rightsizing a board of directors. Individual board cultures vary greatly, but there are two potent tools at a leader's disposal. The first tool lies in the power of a heart-to-heart talk. Always a private session between a board leader and a marginal member, this approach starts with an honest presentation of the problem. Especially when it occurs in tandem with some message from the organization's environment—say, an unexpected threat to a revenue source—this move will often accomplish exactly what is intended.

The second tool comes in handy when the first fails: the power of old-fashioned negotiation. Often the rewards an individual gains from board membership—prestige, visibility, contacts—can be provided just as easily in some other way without full-fledged voting membership. A bit of creative thinking can go far in this vein. In all cases, however, it is important not to let the individual(s) break their ties with the organization completely. The goal is to shift the location of the tie from the board level to a more appropriate vehicle.

The stakes in keeping boards at the right size are high. One group I know operated with an extraordinarily large board for many years.

Over a period of about three months, a major funding source threatened to pull out, revealing that the years of muddled leadership had missed major signals of dissatisfaction. Suddenly the organization was in a crisis and had to fight for its very existence. It should be noted that small board size guarantees nothing about effectiveness, rather it merely sets the stage for it. How to increase the board's effectiveness is a matter for another day.

For a nonprofit, big is beautiful for the spirit, but bad for the board.

The Natural Laws of Task Forces, Committees, and Boards of Directors

"If the Minutemen had formed a task force, we'd be British subjects today."

—Anonymous

An inescapable reality of any nonprofit manager's job is task forces, whether they take the form of committee meetings or boards of directors. All of these groups exist to accomplish a specific task or set of tasks. The only significant difference is their intended life expectancy and whether the task is legally required or is just agreed upon.

Happily, most task groups are fairly predictable. So we developed a few principles for analyzing and predicting their behavior. Keep them in mind for when the occasion rises.

PRINCIPLES FOR TASK FORCES

The leadership core of any task force is never greater than the square root of its total membership.

Try this law out in any task group you know. In a task force of 10, no more than 3 people hold the power. In a group of 25, it's held by 5 or fewer people, and so on. This means that you can write off most of a task group's membership when it comes to influencing future directions. Go for the leadership core and forget about the rest. Note that the leadership core is expressed as a maximum. In a group of 10, there could be as few as two leaders. Or even one. Or zero.

We have no idea exactly why this principle works. It probably has something to do with the fact that there is a limited amount of room for leaders in any group, and no amount of cramming and shoe-horning is going to change it. This has enormous implications for managing a board of directors. Mostly it means that, when you are attempting to get something passed, you need only identify the leaders and get their support. The others will come naturally, because the leaders are the ones everyone looks to for cues as to how to think, behave, and vote. It's not that a board can't have more than its square root's worth of natural leaders—many boards boast a number of people who are unequalled leaders in their own fields—but rather that leadership in this context is a matter of timing. Also, leadership is not just a matter of position on the board. It comes from a delicate blend of position, personality, credibility, experience, ideas, character, and a few other ingredients known only to mystics and management school professors.

The half-life of the average task force is about six months.

Like radioactive material, task forces lose their potency after a period of time. People change jobs or shift emphases in their existing jobs, departments get reorganized, task force members leave and join late, etc. A serious implication of this law: If the average half-life is six months, then after one year only 25 percent of the original potency remains. After 18 months, it's down to 12.5 percent and still declining. See the problem? A task force never ends.

Corollary to the above: Task force issues are neither created nor destroyed, they're simply passed on to other task forces.

Take no task force seriously unless it has a copier assigned to it.

With the possible exception of initial public offerings, no business undertaking routinely causes as much deforestation as a good solid task force. Everyone needs a copy of everything. Then there are the reports. Most task forces issue preliminary reports, interim reports, draft final reports, final reports, and an occasional report on the report. Sincere task force sponsors provide for a means of copying and disseminating all this paper. Therefore, the absence of a copier means that no one really wants the task force to work. Don't take this point too literally. Task forces need tools, and copiers are just one kind of tool. Depending on the size and nature of the task force, other tools may be needed too, such as staff hours, funds for consultants, travel expenses, etc.

Task force co-directors never work.

Two steering wheels only work on big fire trucks.

A successful task force is run like a Christmas tree.

A good task force is run the way big farm families of the nineteenth century used to decorate their Christmas trees. Every member gets to put on at least one favored rule, regulation, provision, or exception. They then return to their clan of origin and point to their contribution as evidence of time well spent. Like parents, the leadership core graciously assents to this method because they control the top levels.

Boards of directors want to hand off power.

Boards of directors are generally happiest when they can hand off power to an executive director or management team they trust. This willingness to delegate seems counter-intuitive. After all, revolutions have been fought for the purpose of gaining power. Politicians do silly things in public to get power, and other people go through entire careers just to have a shot at a few years on the CEO throne. So why would boards of directors be willing to hand off their power?

There are several reasons. First, the stakes are pretty low. No director has a financial investment in the nonprofit, and any prestige that membership might confer is fleeting and hard to measure. Second, most people approach the job from the outside—they see themselves as community representatives rather than aspiring internal managers. Third, many people familiar with for-profit business are just not comfortable with what they see as the foreign culture of a nonprofit. Fourth, few board members can figure out what it is they're supposed to be doing anyway, so the safer course of action is to delegate.

Corollary to the above: Micromanagement is a sign that the board does not trust the CEO.

Boards will only delegate if they trust the executive director to do the job and get it done right. If they mistrust the person, the natural tendency is to do more of it themselves. This is called micromanaging.

CONCLUSION

Nonprofit organizations of all kinds face unprecedented challenges. A careful reading of history and economics tells us that in this type of hostile, fast-changing environment, organizations face a fundamental choice: perish or form a task force.

You can vote on it.

In Praise of Hidden Government Subsidies

Running just about any corporation today means having to be good at market research, financial management, information processing, and many other specialties. Since few organizations can succeed at all these things, they need outside help. When for-profit managers find a reliable partner to provide services they're regarded as shrewdly effective. Nonprofit managers enjoy the benefits of outside advisors too. Often those advisors are called the government. This is one of the reasons why nonprofit overhead rates can be lower than comparable for-profits.

Subsidies often come in the form of a check ready to be cashed. But the really interesting subsidies are the ones that come in the form of a service or an administrative model. We recently had the opportunity to work with a nonprofit vocational services agency that prided itself on deriving a significant portion of its revenue from subcontracted work with private industry. A few years ago, the organization made a major investment in real estate and equipment designed to substantially increase its capacity to produce this subcontract work. Within two years, it was painfully evident that the major investment was a major mistake, and that the future of the entire entity was threatened as a result.

What caused this problem? In management terms, nothing very unusual. Companies overestimate their ability to sell products or deliver their services every day. In fact, even as this is being written, the company that made my computer is staggering under the burden of excess inventory caused by its failure to accurately predict personal computer purchasing trends. There is, however, a price to be paid for failing to accurately identify market trends. In the case of the vocational services agency we mentioned, the price may be more than it can afford. Having overestimated the size of its market, the agency has made investment decisions which have rendered it unable to meet its next payroll or payroll tax obligations.

For the nonprofit manager, the significance of this situation is *not* that a nonprofit brought itself to the brink of ruin by failing to properly assess its market. Rather, the critical point is that many other nonprofits never attempt to assess their markets. Is this because nonprofit managers are smarter and simply do not need to conduct market analyses? Unfortunately, no. It is because government funders supply a lot of hidden subsidies, and market research is one of them.

THE GOVERNMENT FUNDER'S UNSPOKEN ROLE

Most nonprofit managers are familiar with governmental agencies as the *writer of checks* for services provided. But it is naïve and simplistic to think that writing checks is all that governments do when they get involved in the provision of services by nonprofits. In addition to the high profile activities such as writing the laws and regulations and deciding what group gets what funds for which purpose, governments also supply a raft of valuable services that their nonprofit partners would otherwise have to provide for themselves.

This happens because units of government, like all bureaucracies, prefer to do business with entities that look like they do. For example, large urban government funders will gravitate to similarly large nonprofit providers of services. Small county human service boards will tend to prefer funding small local agencies. For the government funder to do its job, it needs to know that its nonprofit partner can work on its level. The result is that it does certain things to help ensure that that happens.

Here are just a handful of the ways that governmental funders provide unacknowledged subsidies of management knowledge, systems, and ideas to nonprofits.

Market Research

Most for-profit companies spend a fair amount of time and resources studying their markets. The larger they are, the more formally they must study their customers. Even a slight misjudgment can cause a loss of real dollars or worse. Larger companies have whole departments dedicated to tracking and analyzing market trends.

For nonprofit agencies it's very different. By the time the nonprofit sector is asked to provide services, the market research has already been done. Often, government entities approach nonprofits to provide services when there is an unmet need in the community that government itself is not equipped to provide. Either the government *is* the market (in which case the market research was just the outcome of a political process), or else it says that the market is there and then backs up the nonprofit service provider by providing money or funding guarantees. Whatever the process, it means that nonprofits' market research never needs to go much further than being able to read the Request for Proposals (RFP). An important note: The government doesn't always call it correctly as far as client needs are concerned. But, right or wrong, the simple act of putting money behind the need automatically creates a market.

Accountability Roadmaps

Nonprofits and government share a common need for accountability to funders. Unlike their for-profit counterparts whose products and services can be fairly easily evaluated and monitored by consumers, the quality of products and services produced by nonprofits and government can be harder to measure. In part this is due to the fact that the recipients of many government and nonprofit services are not the same as the purchasers of those products and services. The result is demands for accountability that exceed those of the IRS. For better or worse, these demands get translated into often elaborate systems for ensuring accountability in such areas as handling money, serving clients, and carrying out research.

The hidden subsidy is that government officials usually spell out exactly how they expect the nonprofit to operationalize accountability goals, often providing forms and policies and even stipulating how the nonprofit is to go about demonstrating its compliance. These are all things that an individual nonprofit would have to spend time and money developing if the government didn't supply them.

Continuous Management Training

An extremely hidden subsidy in many government/nonprofit relationships is continuous management training provided by bureaucrats but disguised as something else (such as regular updates on compliance requirements). Small nonprofits doing business with government agencies will usually have only one or two managers (like the executive director) who are knowledgeable about the terms of the relationship. When that manager leaves the agency, his or her successor has to rebuild or learn the intricacies of the partnership. This costs time and money. Wise government officials realize that it's in their best interest to supply a lot of that knowledge firsthand in the form of on-the-job-training (of course, this can work in the other direction too).

Administrative Recipe Cards

When I first became an executive director of a small nonprofit many years ago I had little practical knowledge of financial management. At the end of my first month I got a crash course in invoicing, courtesy of the local government funder who knew she had to train me quickly or else her own financial records would have fallen hopelessly behind. Thereafter, my staff and I also learned many things about financial recordkeeping, information management, and even corporate restructuring. Even if we could have found the same information through traditional courses and training sessions—a doubtful proposition—it would have cost us a lot of money.

Information Technology

Increasingly, government is subsidizing nonprofits through information technology. Most often this takes the form of the government paying for the development of standardized reporting systems of some kind. Related to this may be having the developer bundle the software with specialized computer or other processing equipment for "turnkey" acquisitions. For instance, some nonprofits have been required to participate in a statewide client service reporting system developed at the government's expense. They were then funded to acquire the necessary software and hardware to run the system, and their training was free. Medicaid and other insurers will sometimes furnish swipe card or other data verification technology that has the same effect.

None of this investment is made by the government with an altruistic motivation. Case managers needed to keep track of their consumers and the services they authorized, as well as when and how the services were actually delivered. So it can be said that the ostensible generosity was really just a way to accomplish the governmental agenda. The real subsidy here—other than developing and funding a way to accomplish a secondary agenda that the nonprofits were interested in anyway—can be described as technology leadership. Providing case management software, a swipe card client verification system or other such innovation indirectly tells the nonprofit recipient that it's time to move to a better operating system, to get proficient in groupware, or simply to upgrade their computer hardware. Leadership in nonprofit technology doesn't often come from within, so government innovation is a reliable way to get it done.

Of course, there are disadvantages to having these unique subsidies. Having such critical functions done by external parties tends to atrophy management muscle. More important, it hides the fact that these are legitimate functions that need to get done. And the services provided by a government office are rarely the exact kind and quality that the nonprofit needs. Still, subsidies are subsidies. Acknowledge them and take advantage of them whenever you can.

The Rise of the ASO

E very now and then an idea comes around that seems so timely, so sensible, so *right* that you find yourself wondering what took it so long and why it hasn't revolutionized everything in its path. Such is the case with something called—well, that's part of the reason why this particular idea has taken so long to come around.

MANY NAMES

The kind of entity that we refer to is called many different things. Some call it an Administrative Services Organization (ASO), some call it Shared Services or a Service Bureau. Still others call it a parent corporation (although we believe that parent corporation implies governance control, while an ASO is based on a contract).

However it's referred to, the central idea is the same. A group of nonprofits gets together to share one or more services that each would otherwise have had to perform separately. This could be anything from preparing paychecks to handling accounting records to computerizing records processing or dozens of other routine administrative tasks. Instead of multiple computer systems, parallel investments, and wasteful duplicate staffs, the organizations gain the benefits of streamlining and greater management sophistication for the same or fewer dollars.

ASOs ARE NOTHING NEW

Administrative services organizations, or ASOs, are nothing new (we'll call them ASOs, but many other names work just as well). Back in the days of old-fashioned risk-sharing/fee-for-service health care plans, some health insurers offered so-called ASO plans to large employers. In return for fixed payments each month, the insurer would lend its name, rate structure, payment collection, and bill payment systems to a big company. The catch was that the company, not the insurer, was fully at risk for the financial performance of the plan—the insurer was selling administrative services only, hence the term ASO.

Corporate America has quietly explored the ASO concept, often calling it *shared services*. Mostly this means figuring out how natural clusters of offices, stores, or factories within a much larger corporate structure can share common overhead resources. *Brownfield* shared services describe arrangements that aim to expand an existing successful operation to handle many different sites beyond its own. *Greenfield* shared services are those that create entirely new service entities. A key difference here is that for-profits create shared services between sites of the same company, not between many different companies as most nonprofits would have to do.

Many common nonprofit situations breed similar arrangements. Not far from my office is a cluster of separate hospitals that get their steam-generated electricity, utilities, and laundry services from a joint corporation set up for just that purpose. The IRS created a category for such organizations. Even joint purchasing arrangements are a form of service-providing association, though usually not involving a separate corporate structure. One trade association set up a joint purchasing program that continues supplying members with everything from insurance to office supplies to furniture to this day.

So ASOs are nothing new. What is new is that increasing fixed costs are prompting many more organizations to join or establish such an arrangement. For many if not most nonprofits today, the fixed cost of providing services is increasing faster than their revenues. Some of those fixed costs include obvious ones like expensive computer equipment and new or rehabilitated buildings. These costs often must be incurred just for the nonprofit to survive.

But there are less obvious types of fixed costs too. Those powerful computer systems need people to keep them going. Many nonprofit organizations today need a director of development, not just a proposal writer as may have been true a decade or two ago. Personnel specialists estimate that any workforce of 25 or more employees usually needs professional human resource (HR) management, and many nonprofits find that their employees' needs are unusually complex. All three types of positions are a substantial piece of overhead that small- to medium-size nonprofits typically cannot afford on their own.

One way of dealing with these needs is to merge nonprofit organizations. While this is a powerful strategy, it is not universally accepted, nor is it universally desirable. This is the vacuum that ASOs are beginning to fill.

WHERE TO FIND ASOs

Where does one find ASOs in the nonhospital nonprofit world today? The answer is everywhere—if you know where to look. ASOs today are being built one brick at a time, such as when a rehabilitation service agency created an insurance trust for fifteen nonprofits in its area. In another example, United Way agencies that do pledge paperwork processing for two or three smaller United Ways are acting as ASOs.

Perhaps the more important question is where one can find ASOs in the future. Judging from what we've seen, ASOs in the future will grow out of these separate, quiet arrangements that are developing today. Rarely will such an entity spring full grown from nothing. Instead, they are likely to develop bit by bit over an extended period of time. It is entirely conceivable that some service-providing organizations today will eventually become strictly ASOs as their management systems become their major source of unique value.

If current economic trends continue, these tentative relationships will need to become much more formalized and explicit as they grow into large, local systems and then link up to serve entire regions. Eventually, some nonprofit sectors may see a nationwide system of regional ASOs.

In things like this, there is a natural tendency to look to trade associations to become ASOs, and in fact some are already beginning to move in this direction. But this is unlikely to become the norm, for reasons that are as subtle as they are compelling. The truth is, most associations don't have much management capability. In economic terms an association is often nothing more than a small business—a handful of employees in a small office with limited management resources. Significantly, many associations don't even have enough employees to qualify for a group health plan, let alone the capacity to manage millions of dollars in administrative services.

ASSOCIATIONS AND FOUNDATIONS ARE CATALYSTS

Still, associations have an essential role as catalysts and planners for the development of ASOs. If an association is not able to supply the services itself, it will need to become skilled at recognizing management achievement and the natural groupings among members that can produce an ASO.

Foundations have a role too. They will need to facilitate an honest discussion of the pressing need for management capacity in nonprofits, only a part of which is the ASO model. They are well-positioned to promote a vision of administrative efficiency and effectiveness in the service of quality programming. And, of course, they'll need to fund particularly promising ASOs.

Occasionally, good ideas are ahead of their time. Other times they're already here, they just don't carry a clear label.

Proactive Management through Benchmarking

I
t often starts with a manager's gut sense, a slowly growing feeling that a particular department is not as efficient
as it might be. Born of observation, the feeling is nurtured
through casual conversations with peers in similar organizations, or
perhaps through an especially useful workshop at a conference. It tugs
on the manager's mind, refusing to be dismissed but hard to substanti-
ate. The unspoken doubt is always the same: *How can I be sure?*

Most managers have had this kind of experience, but until recently
most have little to guide them in acting on it beyond hunches and
seat-of-the-pants estimates. Today, dramatically improved information processing capabilities have combined with increasingly standardized reporting in certain sectors to allow some nonprofits to find
or develop benchmarks useful in operations management matters.

St. John's Manor, a nonprofit nursing home in the Northeast, successfully used benchmarks to assess and reorganize one of its most
important departments. St. John's experience illustrates the power of
benchmark analysis in improving efficiency and it offers a workable
model that others can simulate in a wide variety of ways. Their use
of this data can be imitated in virtually any type of department—or
an entire agency—with similarly powerful results.

THE DEPARTMENT IN THE BEGINNING

The dietary department of St. John's has a familiar responsibility:
produce three daily meals, often to doctor's orders, for dozens of

Table 2

St. John's Manor		All Homes	For Profit	Non-Profit	150–199 Beds	Region 5
Dietary	17.44	10.42	10.22	12.88	11.05	11.26

elderly residents. The mandate is to do it on time, do it accurately, and do it with grace and respect for the residents as individuals. Dietary department staff take pride in their work, often pointing to the quality of their food service as a distinguishing factor that sets St. John's apart from other area facilities.

But reimbursement for long-term care is changing rapidly. In the past, the reimbursement system allowed quality to be produced at virtually any cost. St. John's managers, however, recognized that today they have to deliver quality while controlling costs. It was increasingly clear that the dietary department was not controlling some of its costs. But which costs were out of line, and by how much? And what could be done about it? The home's managers used these questions for benchmark analysis.

Fortunately, St. John's operates in a state requiring detailed cost and utilization reports from its nursing homes. By obtaining these public records, St. John's was able to compare its overall dietary department performance with that of its peers. The results are shown in Table 2.

St. John's first step was to compare its dietary department costs with all nursing homes in the state, then with all nonprofit nursing homes. The second comparison was with facilities of approximately the same size. Finally, St. John's compared itself with all nursing homes in the region. All data in the tables are expressed as costs per patient day to facilitate comparisons.

As Table 2 indicates, St. John's costs were higher than industry practices. The next step was to "drill down" to compare the components of overall dietary cost. Table 3 summarizes these findings. As one can see, St. John's ranked high in all components of dietary cost.

SKEPTICS REMAIN

Some dietary staff remained unconvinced. Everyone knew that St. John's was a flagship facility, they said, and all of these numbers were the average of many homes large and small. A more focused com-

Table 3

St. John's Manor		All Homes	For Profit	Non- Profit	150–199 Beds	Region 5
Salaries	9.44	5.70	5.35	6.54	5.49	5.88
Food	6.33	4.16	4.10	4.36	4.10	4.42
Purchased services	0.00	0.38	0.13	1.13	0.78	0.35
Dietician	0.37	0.26	0.24	0.26	0.03	0.09
Supplies	1.30	0.52	0.49	0.64	0.58	0.59
Total dietary	16.14	11.02	10.31	12.93	10.98	11.33

Table 4

Other Homes

St. Johns Manor		A	B	C	D	E
Salaries	9.44	7.95	6.43	5.83	7.89	8.53
Food	6.33	5.41	4.89	4.91	4.48	3.93
Purchased services	0.00	0.14	0.00	0.00	0.00	0.00
Dietician	0.37	0.00	0.00	0.00	0.00	0.00
Supplies	1.30	1.02	0.94	0.60	1.22	0.57
Total Dietary	16.14	14.52	12.26	11.34	13.59	13.24

parison using similarly positioned nursing homes would narrow the gap. For instance, a number of similar-size nonprofit homes were strongly ethnic, and although St. John's did not serve an ethnic menu, its own high standards imposed comparably high costs. Surely their dietary costs would be in line with a more precise sample.

Using a relational database software program, consultants were able to devise a third benchmark analysis based on a handful of homes selected by St. John's staff. This time no more room for skepticism remained. Table 4 shows that, by all comparisons, St. John's was clearly a high-cost producer. Analysis showed that just about all of its dietary functions cost more than almost all of its peers.

WHAT NEXT?

It is worth remembering that St. John's undertook this analysis on its own, without any pressure from outside forces such as funders or regulators. One of the rewards of St. John's proactive approach was the ability to solve the problem on its own terms. After careful analysis of the benchmarks, dietary department managers and staff devised a two-part plan.

First, they reviewed their purchasing and materials handling practices. Concluding that some major suppliers had been overcharging them, they put their food and supplies purchasing contracts out to bid. In the process, they also revised some of their food receiving and accounting practices. Estimated savings from this effort alone were in the $.75–1.00 per patient day range, enough to bring them within a respectable distance of industry norms.

The second step, reorganizing staffing patterns, was harder. After all, the very people who had been involved in the problem-solving process could theoretically lose their jobs. With the agreement of senior management, they resolved to impose a hiring freeze on their department and reduce staff costs through attrition.

Predictably, the payoff for this strategy has been slower. More aggressive staff reductions may still be necessary in the future. But a secondary and more subtle benefit has come from the benchmarking activity. Today, the dietary department has generated greater internal respect from other departments which themselves are struggling with similar issues. Other departments are considering using process simulation to reengineer their production processes, and have gained a good reputation for themselves. Their participatory style and objective problem-solving approach, all supported by senior management, have set new standards for the entire organization. And that is one gain that can't be benchmarked.

Giving Diligence Its Due

Recently one of our nonprofit clients was approached by another nonprofit with a merger proposal. The other nonprofit executive director had a clear plan in mind that involved turning over quite a bit of everyday operations to our client, while retaining for his own concentration certain programs and services for which he would be responsible as a program manager.

The possibility was tempting. Our client is well-run, strategically minded, and poised for growth. They had already discussed the possibility of merging and were prepared for such a proposal. But a cursory financial review surfaced two or three significant areas of concern. One of these concerns was expected, but the other two were not. What to do?

Perhaps if our client had been a publicly held corporation with a long history of taking over other companies, the next step would have been second nature. In nonprofit management, however, the idea of mergers is only slowly being accepted. Although the numbers of agencies considering merger is increasing dramatically, many have not even completed a single merger and many more have yet to consider one. For an agency in this position the next step is to conduct a due diligence investigation.

WHY A DUE DILIGENCE INVESTIGATION?

One of the cardinal rules of nonprofit mergers and strategic alliances is to know one's partner. Generally nonprofits considering some form of merging or alliance-building already know at least the bare minimum about their prospective partner. Unlike for-profit companies where a merger can occur between companies on both coasts as easily as it can between companies in the same city, nonprofits are typically rooted in a specific local area and their relationships occur accordingly. This means that they usually know something about a prospective partner well before the process begins. The early stages of a merger or alliance involve a high-level confirmation of that knowledge.

The potential problem with this scenario is that it can provide a false sense of security based on incomplete or erroneous information. At some point, the prospective partners must dig deeper into each other's operations. Typically this will happen partway into the process when the broad outlines of an agreement have been worked out but the implementation has not yet begun. The point is to learn things that may change the agreement at a time when it is early enough to incorporate them.

Due diligence as a term has a very legalistic sound, and for good reason. When owners' and investors' money is at stake it is not only a very good idea but in many cases a legal requirement that managers be *duly diligent* in documenting what they know about their partner. Many transactions have fallen through or been substantially modified on the basis of a due diligence investigation.

No fortunes are at stake in a nonprofit merger or strategic alliance. Why should these participants perform a due diligence? The fact that private wealth will be unaffected by a nonprofit transaction is unimportant. The surviving corporate structure will often have to assume the liabilities of its partner. Some liabilities in a nonprofit carry more weight than others. Unpaid tax bills, for instance, can result in legal action against boards of directors as individuals. And we would argue that assuming certain types of liabilities is a moral responsibility for an organization seeking to serve the public good, even if it is not legally required. In both instances it is essential for the new board of directors and management to know what they will be assuming responsibility for. Finally, even in the absence of any legal implications, a due diligence investigation will produce significant operational detail that managers need to know once they assume the new responsibility.

HOW IT WORKS

Some managers assume that a due diligence is largely financial in nature. While it is true that a good deal of the material covered is financial, if finances were the only aspect a due diligence covered it could be accomplished by a financial analysis and a peek at the back-room systems. In practice, there will be some overlap between the initial explorations conducted by a nonprofit considering a merger or alliance and the more formal process of a due diligence investigation. (See Figure 8.)

In addition to these areas, we have found that other areas are equally important, such as:

- Does it make sense for these organizations to get together?
- Is there a cultural "fit" between them?
- Are the organizations strategically complementary?
- Will the new management and personnel be able to handle increased size?

The quantitatively oriented part of the process will often—although not always—confirm liabilities that the organization knew about. Sometimes interviews with key staff will reveal real or potential liabilities about which senior management or the board was unaware. For example, a review of insurance policies may disclose a gap in coverage for a period of time in the past. If a claim surfaces after the alliance or merger is consummated it may have to be handled by the new organization. In any agency that bills for its services, especially in complicated areas involving third party coverage, the valuation of its outstanding invoices may change greatly when a knowledgeable new party reviews them.

Who should perform a due diligence investigation? This is one of those areas where the determinedly self-reliant nonprofit will want to do it in-house. For many reasons, this is not a good idea. In-house staff may or may not be adequately skilled to perform due diligence work and will rarely have current experience at it. For that reason they will probably be sloppy and inefficient. There is also the distinct possibility of bias in the outcome. Having an outside party do the due diligence makes for better accountability if something goes wrong. Generally, due diligence investigations are carried out by some combination of outside accountants and attorneys.

An old proverb says that in any transaction "the buyer needs a thousand eyes, the seller only one." While there are no buyers or sellers in the technical sense in a nonprofit alliance, the board and

General

Articles of incorporation
By-laws
Recent minutes of board meetings
Relevant licenses and permits

Financial

Audited financial statements for the previous three to five years
Contracts (as both buyer and supplier) and leases
Debt instruments, if any
Annual budget for the past two years and future year
Program budgets for same periods
Accounts receivable analysis
Accounts payable analysis
Information about capital assets
Current status of tax obligations
Insurance policies
Information about restricted funds, if any
Information about pending litigation
Information about current or recent government audits
Regulatory filings
Copies of fundraising material

Personnel

Salary schedule, including full-time equivalencies
List of active employees
Information about benefits package
Personnel policies
Collective bargaining information, if applicable
Pending claims (overtime, unpaid wages)
History of workers' compensation claims
Unemployment claim history

From: "Seven Steps to a Successful Nonprofit Merger," *T. McLaughlin, National Center for Nonprofit Boards (Washington, DC, 1996).*

Figure 8.   Areas for a Due Diligence Investigation

management that will eventually assume the full range of liabilities will want to make sure that they know what the liabilities are. One could even say that both boards have a fiduciary duty to know the details about a larger and surviving merger partner.

Due diligence is one of those vaguely official sounding terms that many nonprofit managers would never expect to encounter. Nevertheless, the opportunities for encountering it are multiplying. As a process, it is fairly straightforward and easy to understand. It can also save time and prevent misunderstandings. It pays to be duly diligent about due diligence.

Related Parties

For-profits have insider trading. Nonprofits have related parties. Both involve undue influence over the affairs of the organization by insiders in conjunction with outside parties. The definition of a related party is not precise. It seems that just about every governmental or quasi-governmental player that has anything to say about defining related party relationships in a nonprofit corporation defines them differently.

The relationship between the sources of related party definitions and the type of provider being regulated is such that, the more generic and broad-based the focus, the more generic the definition of related party. The more specific and narrow the regulator's concern, the more stringent the definition. There is also a more telling inverse relationship—the weaker the political and economic clout of those being regulated, the greater the specificity of the definition.

Similar patterns apply when it comes to deciding what to do about the existence of a related party relationship. Essentially, the American Institute of Certified Public Accountants (AICPA) prescribes disclosure. At the other end of the spectrum, some units of government also insist on disclosure, but go on to spell out a series of additional steps that could potentially have a serious economic effect on willful violators.

At the heart of these patterns, of course, are matters of power and control. Providers of service usually establish related parties because they offer some degree of increased control over their financial affairs. Government purchasers try to limit related parties in order to maximize their control over contractors. Considering that government can no longer provide many services directly and that most nonprofit organizations would be hobbled without government money, it's probably a healthy tension.

The critical point is reached when the nonprofit's establishment of related parties goes beyond being a recognized means of dealing with, say, a quirky reimbursement system and becomes instead a means of personal enrichment. The problem is that this is where the similarities between nonprofit and for-profit stop.

The majority shareholder who steers his company in the direction of a major transaction with another of his holdings is not necessarily doing anything wrong. The nonprofit board member who does the same thing violates the spirit of his duties and perhaps even a regulation or a law. The responsibility of outside directors on a corporate board is to represent the stockholders. In a sense, the nonprofit board is composed of exclusively "outside" directors since their job is in part to represent the public.

In the end, there will always be related parties because the right to choose one's business partners is so fundamental, even for nonprofits for whom the mechanics of business are secondary to their purpose. Equally as certain is the need for nonprofit managements and boards to recognize fully the narrow area which constitutes the bounds of acceptable related party agreements.

Down With Geography, Or Why You Have Service Gaps

Pick a national organization of nonprofit agencies. Pick any organization—it probably doesn't matter. Choose a household name, one that is as easily recognized in Dubuque as in Denver or Detroit. Now look at the services it provides through its affiliates in any geographic area across the country. Chances are you will find many areas where comparable, nonaffiliated agencies provide far more services or are more far-reaching than the local branch of the national organization. From the point of view of the national organization, these are service gaps and they represent weak points in their system.

Why is this the case? Figure 9 tries to get at part of the answer. The larger circle represents the service needs of the geographic area staked out by the local affiliate, and usually agreed to by the national sponsor. Within this defined geographic area is a more or less identifiable set of needs that, at least theoretically, could be filled by the local nonprofit. The smaller circle represents the proportion of services the affiliate actually provides.

The discrepancy between needs and services actually provided can be explained in many ways, but most of them are only retrospective explanations. The most profound explanation is that the local affiliate voluntarily defined its own service and geographic niche many years ago, ceding the rest of their territory to whatever other groups wanted it.

So if a local affiliate decides—as it is almost certain to do—to concentrate on only a portion of the needs that it might serve, the rest of its geographic territory's service needs will either go unmet

Figure 9.   Service Needs of Geographic Area

or be covered by others. This kind of choice is almost inevitable when the services are complex and widespread. It is difficult to offer a wide range of programs with equal effectiveness, and so organizations tend naturally to specialize in only one or two. They also tend to specialize in specific populations.

One might ask what's wrong with this situation. From a public service perspective, as long as legitimate public needs get met in some fashion, there's not much wrong. But for individual nonprofits, and for any national system of which they might be a part, it leads to organizational weakness.

Here's why. Organizing by geography practically demands competition when the nonprofit "owner" of the territory refuses even to attempt to serve the entire area. Staking out a large geographic area—the large circle in the figure—and then not serving it completely leaves huge gaps. This is what happens when "Agency X of Greater Dogwood" is really more like Agency X of the North Side of Dogwood. Who is going to serve the other three points of the Dogwood compass? And what about the folks unlucky enough to live outside of Dogwood?

Government funding sources are notorious for defining service areas geographically. Remember catchment areas in the health care field? Even in the parts of the country where these still exist, participants tend to regard them as the faint footprints of 1960s and 1970s social planning.

But the real commitment to organizing geographically often comes from nonprofit managers themselves. As entities that came about in part to deal with some sort of dysfunction in the larger society, nonprofits are fiercely local creatures. They often rightfully become magnets for community pride, and any attempt to expand their geographic identification runs into strong resistance. In the end, others come in to fill the gaps, and the local provider that began with such strong local ties becomes trapped as others fill the void— or, worse, as those deserving service go without.

This is one reason that for-profit competitors can pose such a major threat to traditionally operated nonprofits. Without geographic ties to restrict them, and with the ability to raise significant capital, some for-profit companies may be able to establish a commanding presence in the areas they target.

GEOGRAPHY IS PROTECTIONISM

At the heart of all this is that geography as an organizing principle is a protectionist strategy. Whether it is a funding source that will only fund groups in the catchment area or the national system that grants exclusive "franchise rights" by geography, the end result is the same. Services are provided by those with a geographic claim, not according to what is best for clients and consumers.

The alternative to land mass as a defining principle is to focus on services and needs (we are only talking about the practices of funding sources and national nonprofits here; completely freestanding local nonprofits don't need to consider the policy implications of how a larger system is organized).

Organizing by services and identified needs is a better way to build the kind of sophisticated service-providing and fundraising systems that will be needed in the twenty-first century. This means nothing short of what we might call the "marketization" of health and human services. Services will be delivered according to what groups best deliver them, not according to the address of their headquarters.

For a hypothetical national organization of youth-serving groups,

Figure 10. Service Needs of Geographic Area

a typical service system might look like Figure 10. Whereas in Figure 9 the geographically defined area was largely unserved by any group connected with the national system, in this service-based model a number of local members offer complementary services knitted together by a shared set of national values and the infrastructure to support it. External competitors seeking entry would then tend to focus on unserved niches, not a wide swath of unserved geography.

For national organizations, organizing local members by the services they deliver would lead them necessarily to focus more attention on those services. They would have to develop standard definitions of success and benchmarking systems for measuring it. Outside of advocacy on a national level their greatest contribution would be the articulation and support of service standards.

Organizing according to services rather than geography also helps integrate services. Focusing on services rather than sheer geography increases the likelihood that providers in a given area will be able to concentrate on doing what they do best, and linkage with another agency will be less threatening because of it.

ONE SMALL PROBLEM . . .

The only problem with this model is that it won't work. At least, it won't work anytime soon. Geographical boundaries are so ingrained, and so easy to think about, that it will take years for an alternative principle to take root. A nonprofit organization's competitive hormones are far more easily stimulated by geographic proximity to another agency than is the urge to integrate services. Perhaps more important, this approach moves much closer to what a true market-based system would look like, and it begins to redefine what we mean when we say "community-based."

Still, it is possible to begin explicitly organizing around services and needs in some small way right now. The first step is for national organizations to recognize how a geographic approach to boundaries saps their strength. The next step is to begin considering how they might challenge the self-defeating tendency to compete through lines on a map rather than through excellence of service. Their role in defining and supporting that excellence in service will ultimately be their biggest contribution to their members and affiliates.

Rethinking the United Way

I f our experience is any guide, United Way organizations around the country are experiencing a boomlet of interest in strategic restructuring. This is potentially significant because, as one of the country's best known national nonprofit systems, the United Way is a leader and opinion shaper. As widely supported entities with typically powerful local ties, United Way agencies enjoy solid credibility with business leaders.

THE THREE TASKS OF A UNITED WAY

In concept, the United Way job can be divided into three tasks: raise money, keep track of it, and give it away. What holds the most promise for local United Way organizations—and the agencies they support—is the tantalizing possibility that restructuring the second and third tasks could bolster the first and result in raising more funds.

The process of raising money in a United Way agency is usually called the campaign. This is the time of the year when United Way organizations (they are separate, independent nonprofits, contrary to common misperceptions) renew their fundraising relationships with local employers and their employees. Although the giving process often occurs year-round through a payroll deduction mechanism, the most intense period of renewal and new account solicitation occurs during the campaign.

Once volunteers and United Way staff secure fundraising commitments, the responsible United Way office must process the paperwork and keep track of the donations as they come in. As nonprofit public charities, United Ways are responsible for the funds they collect. This task is more complex than might be apparent, since there are a large number of variables to account for. It could almost be said that no two donors are alike.

Distributing funds to local agencies is often called the allocation process. This process can be carried out in a wide variety of ways, with more or less structure behind it depending on the size of the particular United Way, the economic and cultural realities of its community, and the management style of its leaders.

The task least likely to change for most United Way agencies is the campaign process. It is the signature activity of the overall United Way system and gives each office its local visibility and market presence. Donors typically want to feel that their local dollars will help meet local needs, and so each United Way campaign has a strong interest in meeting that expectation.

IT'S A FINANCIAL SERVICE

The keeping-track-of-it function will change the most for the same reason that virtually all financial services have changed in recent years. Processing pledges and documenting allocations is no different from the kinds of things that credit unions, banks, and financial services firms do every day. And that is the key to restructuring United Ways.

The cost of carrying out many financial services is decreasing due to technology and new ways of doing tasks (consider the productivity gains brought about by spreadsheets, calculators, and automatic teller machines). This function for many large financial services organizations is leading them to create large facilities and massive computer capabilities in low-rent areas to house massive transaction-processing operations.

The "backroom" operations of a United Way office are like small versions of these transaction-processing factories. Historically, each United Way office was expected to be a clone of every other United Way office. But that assumption is now being revisited.

Why should every United Way office, no matter how small or large, invest in staff and technology for doing the same tasks that every other United Way office is expected to do? For smaller offices especially, this is an unreasonably high overhead burden. The effort to increase staff for routine administrative tasks is always draining, doubly so when the organization is too small in the first place. Worse, an hour of staff time spent on administration is an hour of fundraising time lost.

THE BEST REASON TO RESTRUCTURE

A model for restructuring United Ways: Keep the campaign intensely local, and centralize as many administrative systems as possible. Create a regional United Way to handle administrative tasks plus marketing and regional development activities. Alternatively, hand over routine administrative chores to a designated United Way office with particularly good systems. No matter what, retain a vital physical presence in each local community.

This is a highly rational proposition. Perhaps too rational. An undefinable part of every United Way relates to community pride, and community pride can easily obscure rational, businesslike logic. Also, collaborating on administrative tasks isn't as easy as it sounds. Standardizing forms processing procedures really means standardizing the way one goes about delivering a service. It may mean changes in personnel and in governance structure. In any case, it certainly means organizational change, and in the absence of a compelling reason to change, the motivation to do so will probably be lacking.

For a high impact reason to do United Way business differently, start with a simple calculation. Divide the total dollars raised by a United Way office by the total number of staff full-time equivalents (FTEs) directly involved in the campaign. Include all measurable portions of all paid staff time from the executive director to the receptionist who schedules the campaign meetings. Don't include time spent on administrative tasks, allocations or any noncampaign related activity. The resulting number will probably be in the hundreds of thousands of dollars or more.

Now imagine what would happen if some of each campaign staff person's time was freed up from routine administrative chores unrelated to the campaign. What would happen if every major campaign person (even if it's only the executive director in a small United Way) could get just one additional workday per week to devote to developing new accounts or raising more from existing ones? The numbers will vary from office to office, but even a small percentage increase in monies raised as a result of this kind of restructuring could yield tens of thousands and even hundreds of thousands of extra dollars. This is what will motivate boards and community leaders more than any savings targets could possibly achieve.

NEEDS ASSESSMENT TOO

That third task of allocations could also benefit from similar treatment. As with the campaign, donors need to feel that dollars raised locally are allocated to local agencies. The actual mechanics of allocating money to recipient agencies typically varies greatly from United Way to United Way. But while the allocation decisions have to be made locally, support for a professional allocation process could be provided regionally. In fact, to run a truly professional allocation process it almost has to be done on a regional basis. Conducting a needs assessment, for example, is the first logical step in compiling an allocation plan responsive to community needs. Although it should be done with a local focus, the methodologies and some of the staff resources are best deployed regionally rather than to have every local office trying to conduct a professional needs assessment process every few years.

As organizations with one foot in the business world and one in the nonprofit world, United Way offices have a unique opportunity to rethink the way they do business. There are even more profound directions for this rethinking to take, but that's a story for another day. Today, most United Way offices have the chance to put a distinctive stamp on their part of the nonprofit world.

Gilt By Association: Why Associations Must Reshape Themselves

Traditionally, a nonprofit organization's association membership transaction goes something like this: The agency pays its membership fee and in return it gets one or more publications, regular conferences, and information about various issues. The association lobbies on its members' behalf, arranges a special deal or two, and tries to do other things that are important to its members. Everybody goes home happy.

Maintaining this scenario depends on stability in three groups: the association itself, its members, and those that fund the members. But, as a quick glance outside the window will confirm, the second and third groups are on the verge of changing dramatically. Here are some of the factors influencing members and their associations:

Changes in government's role. Government at all levels is backpedaling away from some of its traditional roles and handing them over to another level of government or any other institution that will accept them. Welfare reform, the 1997 Balanced Budget Act, and the failure of the Clinton health plan in 1993 all symbolize the beginning of the federal government's diminishing role in the nation's health and social services system. States will have to pick up the slack, and many of them are experimenting with devolution's close cousin, privatization. The result will mean more opportunities (and pressure) for nonprofits, and a diminished or altered lobbying need for their Washington-based associations.

Increased payor management. Whether it's called capitation, managed care, or something else, payers of all kinds are learning how to manage their purchase of services more tightly. In addition, the private managers—largely insurance and specialized management services companies—are themselves consolidating and restructuring. Management of services is becoming a growth industry.

Nonprofit mergers. Many nonprofits are merging with each other in an attempt to gain everything from market share and improved capitalization to economies of scale and more sophisticated management. These are associations' members, and their mergers will have an impact.

Easier access to information. In the past, associations could tout their access to information and specialized knowledge. While political acumen and physical presence in the centers of power will always matter, the rest of the information that associations typically managed is growing easier to obtain through the Internet and improved computer-assisted communication in general.

The impact on nonprofits from all of these changes is just beginning. In response, they are exploring new ways of organizing themselves, trying to deliver reliably high-quality services while achieving greater economies, and looking for new strategic directions. It is logical, then, that the associations who count these nonprofits as members will also begin to change.

Consider merging. Your members are doing it, so you should consider it too. Although this step is more easily undertaken only after collaboration on one or more of the other three levels, it is already happening in some instances.

Align incentives. This is a fancy way of saying that if you are a single corporation, as a few associations are, act like it. Use the inherent power in this structure to position the whole entity for the future. If not, make sure all members have a reason to follow your program. Don't be shy about stipulating the way your members ought to organize their own corporate structures (mergers, regionalization, etc.) so as to better support your common goals.

Be prepared to get involved in members' management. This may sound frightening now, but some associations will need to assume more responsibility for management and less for advocacy (see economics and responsibility below). And do it up front. It's better to be involved as architects than as firemen.

Get good at market research. This is one area where national or statewide associations can usually mount a more sophisticated research effort than any of their members can. Fundraising is a case in point.

Set program standards. In the system as it has existed so far, programs are developed by local units with little or no communication with others. The result is an enormously vibrant program innovation system, but one which cannot speak to itself. On the level of operations or program management, associations will need to assume the role of definer of programs and performance standards. They can do this by establishing the standards themselves or by working closely with accrediting bodies to endorse theirs.

Either way, associations that develop some sort of performance standards—and the mechanisms to enforce them—will have a huge influence on the quality of their members' programming, not to mention a hammerlock on success.

Industrialize program delivery. Next, associations need to figure out how to get their members to mass-produce the programs they have just defined. Market forces demand standardization in the services they purchase.

Provide benchmarks. No group is in a better position to research and provide benchmarks for services to help members gauge their performance. Descriptive benchmarks—simply compiling a database of what exists out there—are hard enough, but don't stop there. Normative benchmarks, or statements of desirable outcomes irre-

Collaborative Conferences

Most associations run one or more annual conferences for their members, but some associations are taking it a step further. Realizing that statewide associations usually cannot compete with the greater reach of national associations, some statewide groups are beginning to run regional conferences. This gives members easier access to information beyond the traditional confines of their own state without the overwhelming nature of massive national conferences. One six-state association rotates the conference site among desirable destinations in each of the states. Planning is decentralized, but coordinating it all is the responsibility of one of the six associations specifically assigned that role, usually for at least a few years at a time.

spective of what currently exists, are most powerful and give your vision some measurability.

Set administrative standards. This activity is huge, encompassing things ranging from computerized information exchange standards to human resource policies. Whatever standards get chosen will depend on the association's unique mission and position. The hardest part of standard setting may be to convince some members of the value of having association-wide standards at all.

Provide some administrative services. In management terms, associations are odd organizations. The nature of serving members would seem to give them an intense internal focus. In reality, they are highly outwardly focused, and their management systems are not necessarily strong. Yet some associations will find an opportunity to provide centralized management services (payroll or wide-area computer networks, for example). In the end, they may opt to do this through either specially created service companies or by creating regional service corporations based on one or two especially strong members' administrative systems.

Arrange large-scale joint purchasing. Associations are ideally positioned to swing large amounts of their members' purchasing to carefully selected vendors, and many already operate active programs. This would be one of the first things that a forward-looking association could try to do, although to be economically significant it would have to be highly coordinated and integrated with goals at the other levels.

Associations must approach their own restructuring as if it were a tapestry. For example, large-scale joint purchasing would have to be mandatory in order to offer any substantial economic impact. If this were the only initiative that the association undertook, it would doubtless anger its members and ultimately it would fail.

But if each member got guaranteed lowest prices, a smoothly operating payroll system, a nationally recognized market identity, and strong marketing support, they might be willing to pledge to uphold performance standards and purchase certain items from predetermined vendors.

For associations, the good news is that little of this should affect traditional revenue streams. Those that are smart about their dues structures (charging members by size rather than a single fee for all members, large and small) should not see significant losses from members' mergers. Some of their new activities could actually produce new sources of revenue.

The hardest part for associations will be to identify and incorporate the new competencies that they will need. Their job will get harder, a bit less connected with government, and a lot more ambiguous. Which is the same thing happening to their members.

The Business of Trade Shows

Trade shows. Row upon row of tables and booths, each one occupied by yet another type of vendor interested in selling you and your fellow conference goers their goods or services. The industrialized world's air-conditioned equivalent of the ancient street bazaar. The next time your industry's association puts on a conference with a trade show, make a point of checking it out. Because the trade show world is changing, and your association may need all the help it can get to retain or maximize this formerly faithful revenue stream.

BIG BUSINESS

Trade shows are big business for tens of thousands of associations in this country. According to the American Society of Association Executives, 63 percent of all associations typically hold a trade show in conjunction with a yearly conference or annual meeting. In 1998, the average square footage devoted to all aspects of trade shows was equivalent to thirty large single-family homes. And those same exhibitors are responsible for an increasingly large percentage of conference revenues.

Typically, exhibitors pay a fee to rent a fixed amount of space and associated services. In return, conference managers usually encourage all attendees to visit the trade show area, and they often help support vendors' visitor maximization strategies such as raffles and giveaways. More lucrative still are sponsorships, or vendor payments made to the association in return for publicity crediting the vendor for providing everything from the featured speaker to that morning's sunrise.

So why is the well-established trade show formula beginning to change? The answer is rooted in those exhibitors. First of all, there are more and more shows trying to appeal to a finite number of vendor/exhibitors. We can attest to this trend personally. At least once every few months, we receive an invitation to exhibit in a trade show that is either brand-new or in its first few years of existence. Usually it is a statewide or regional conference, and often the conference itself has only been in existence for a few years. These can be less successful because vendors can only cover so many conferences without diluting their impact.

But the major reason has to do with changes in the structure and the needs of the exhibitors themselves. Marketing is a hugely inexact process. Often the success of a product depends not on its quality but on the nature of its distribution system. It is widely accepted that the IBM PC was a world-class success in the early 1980s not because of its quality but because IBM had a superior distribution system.

To run any kind of a marketing program, vendors have to incur large fixed costs. In addition to hiring staff (an enormous form of fixed cost), vendors must absorb the cost of designing and producing marketing materials. Then there are the specific marketing projects themselves, which will demand more or less expenditures depending on what they are.

THE COSTS OF ATTENDING ARE FIXED

The cost of attending trade shows is a very large fixed cost for vendors. They often must invest in a professional-looking booth as well as specialized equipment. Each appearance at a trade show requires a minimum number of staff, professionally prepared materials, and a myriad of other expensive needs. The transportation, lodging, and setup costs alone are generally substantial.

In return, vendors want easy access to large numbers of exactly the right people. This formula is simple, but nonnegotiable. Large numbers of attendees are insufficient; they must be the right ones. This means the attendees must be the prime buyers or the influential people in buying decisions in their own organizations. Textbook sellers want to get in front of school administrators and purchasing agents, pharmaceutical salespeople want physicians and nurses, and so on. Without plenty of these natural matches, the show will be a waste of time for the vendors.

Another more subtle dynamic intensifies this trend. Many for-profit companies are merging with former competitors to create larger business entities. The result is that the decision-maker who formerly supported a particular conference may now need to seek permission to attend it based on a regional marketing strategy developed by a distant corporate office. This also tends to reduce the possibility for sponsorships for small local groups and increase them for larger regional or national meetings.

What we are seeing now is a tendency for vendors to rethink their trade show appearances. While some associations are enjoying record growth in their trade shows, others are being squeezed by vendors who are making it clear that, for whatever reason, their future attendance is not certain. Other associations are just beginning to get into the trade show marketplace. Recently we were approached by an association that had just decided to run a trade show three months before its conference. Even if we had been inclined to exhibit—we weren't, because of a fundamental mismatch between attendees and our desires—we simply could not arrange the mechanics with so little notice.

SHOULD YOUR ASSOCIATION RUN A TRADE SHOW?

The answer to this question is almost always a qualified yes. The profitability of a trade show speaks for itself, although if one factors in the estimated value of association staff time, the real profitability of most conferences shrinks dramatically. Still, there are intangible benefits to be enjoyed, such as greater visibility, a more professional image for the association, and a sense of leadership and market desirability.

There are four things to keep in mind to help ensure a successful trade show for your association's conference or annual meeting.

INCREASE ATTENDANCE THROUGH MARKETING

Your vendors want more attendees, and so do you. The best way to guarantee more attendees is through a coordinated, association-wide marketing campaign. Every decision, ranging from where and when to have the conference to the number and type of speakers, should support the marketing effort. For example, the majority of conference planners send out their conference brochure at least twice—better to send extra copies than to have a potential attendee decide that the hassle of finding that single copy of the brochure isn't worth the benefit of attending the conference.

Sophisticated marketing also uses other association meetings, publications, subcommittees, mailing stamps, voicemail reminders, broadcast faxes, and numerous other techniques to build up attendance. Conference marketing is a year-round activity.

MATCH ATTENDEES WITH VENDOR NEEDS

Inventory software vendors feel distinctly out of place at an art therapists' conference. By being extremely clear about the intended audience, conference presenters can increase the satisfaction of both vendors and attendees and therefore maximize revenue. This isn't as easy as it sounds. Many nonprofit conferences deliberately try to accommodate all types of people typically found in their members' organizations. There is also frequently an egalitarian approach to nonprofit management that blurs distinctions that vendors would rather be sharper. The result can be an unsuccessful trade show where few vendors find adequate numbers of attendees even vaguely interested in their offerings.

MAKE TRADE SHOW ATTENDANCE EASY

Vendors may bring seemingly easy revenue to a conference, but they require some care and feeding. Often they will be far more skilled and experienced at trade shows than a conference's sponsor, since they typically exhibit many times each year. They know what they need, they know what to expect, and a conference which doesn't deliver for them risks not getting them back.

CONSIDER REGIONALIZING YOUR CONFERENCE AND TRADE SHOW

In industries ranging from nursing homes to veterinarians, exhibitors are forcing regional collaborations. Statewide associations, realizing that they cannot compete with the national conferences in their field, are beginning to pool their resources to create regional conferences with enough attendees to retain high-paying vendors while getting better programs and speakers than any of them could afford on their own. This is another area of nonprofit collaboration that will be seeing increased attention in the coming years.

PART FIVE

Resources

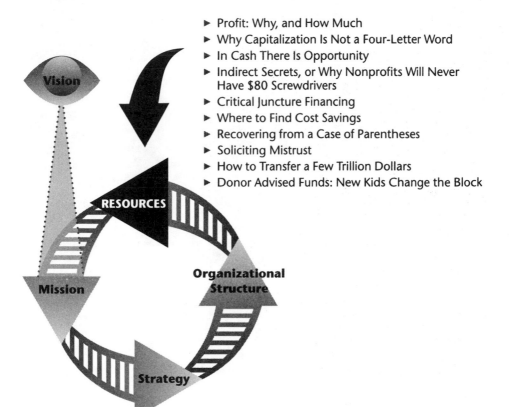

- ▶ Profit: Why, and How Much
- ▶ Why Capitalization Is Not a Four-Letter Word
- ▶ In Cash There Is Opportunity
- ▶ Indirect Secrets, or Why Nonprofits Will Never Have $80 Screwdrivers
- ▶ Critical Juncture Financing
- ▶ Where to Find Cost Savings
- ▶ Recovering from a Case of Parentheses
- ▶ Soliciting Mistrust
- ▶ How to Transfer a Few Trillion Dollars
- ▶ Donor Advised Funds: New Kids Change the Block

Profit: Why, and How Much?

One of the biggest misconceptions in the nonprofit world has to do with the role of profit. Many seem to think that the term itself means that the organizations cannot make a profit. This is untrue. Instead, they simply are not allowed to have shareholders to share the profits with, so the funds "stay inside" the nonprofit corporation. Worse, there is a kind of tacit agreement not to discuss the matter in public, as though it deserved no informed debate. The result is that those connected with nonprofit organizations—consumers, funders, regulators, and even some managers—have no shared vocabulary and no common understanding about this financial need that nevertheless requires careful attention and management.

The importance of profit to a nonprofit is heightened because nonprofits have fewer ways of growing. One way is to borrow long-term funds, such as a mortgage. The other way to boost the financial dimensions of *any* type of corporation is to get an outsider to give money directly to it. In the for-profit world this kind of money is given in exchange for a share of ownership.

Since nonprofit organizations cannot have individual shareholders this method of raising funds is off limits. The nonprofit counterpart is grants. The only way to get money into a nonprofit corporation without the explicit expectation of a financial return (as in borrowing) is through fundraising. A philanthropic term for that strategy is the *capital campaign*, designed to raise a set amount of money in a fixed period of time. In effect, the capital campaign is the equivalent of a stock offering of a for-profit company: a major, orchestrated attempt to sell all or part of the organization to the general public. The difference is that major donors, unlike major stockholders, can get no promise of control or direct economic value in exchange for their money. Any benefits they do receive, such as public recognition, may, in fact, have value but it is incidental to the transaction.

These simple facts create a serious structural blockage to adequate capitalization in a nonprofit corporation. If selling shares in the entity is forbidden and if a capital campaign is unrealistic—as it is for many nonprofits—then there will be extra pressure on the two remaining ways of bringing in capital, borrowing and profits.

Internally generated profits are the major capital source under the routine control of the nonprofit manager. There is no practical alternative. This puts enormous pressure on the organization's internal management controls to produce a surplus on a regular basis, while simultaneously negotiating internal political crosscurrents around profitability. The pivotal question—how much profit is enough?—is intimately linked to the uses to which that profit will be put. To no one's surprise, the uses of profit in a nonprofit corporation are exactly the same as those in a for-profit organization, except to make its owners wealthy.

Profit for stability is probably the most common and easily understood use for profits in a nonprofit. For a corporation with adequate and reliable funding and good systems, stability created by profitability can mean the ability to concentrate on mission without energy-draining fiscal distractions.

Another use for profit is personnel bonuses. There is nothing illegal about this practice even though it raises the aura of ethical concerns for some. In part this is due to the quaint but still-prevalent notion that those who work in a nonprofit organization of any kind must be motivated by the pleasures of the work itself and not by the filthy lucre.

Profit for innovation is a third and somewhat foreign concept because there is usually no incentive for a nonprofit to innovate. But in the twenty-first century, the pressure will be on nonprofits to innovate. Until the 1990s, nonprofits generally had been buffered from the effects of innovation typical of industry because it normally occurred in areas of technology or middle management, neither of which nonprofit organizations use in abundance. However, in the future the pressure to innovate will come to direct services (in some areas it already has), and the intelligent nonprofit will be prepared.

Finally, we have profit for growth. Growth in any field means having enough cash available to seize opportunities or cushion unexpected losses. Generating profits can help tremendously.

Of course, growth in a nonprofit whose mission is to serve the public means something fundamentally different than growth in a for-profit company. Action for Children's Television, a legendary nonprofit dedicated to reforming children's television, never grew much at all in a financial sense. Its growth was entirely programmatic and political in nature, as it came to be seen for many years as the dominant, credible voice in the campaign to reform children's commercial TV.

Still, for many, if not most, organizations, growth in ability to accomplish mission usually entails growth in a financial sense too. In fact, for many types of public service the two are inseparable. For them, growth in the financial dimension should be seen not as the by-product but as the necessary precondition to growth in mission.

There is no better way to prepare for a given level of profit than an informed discussion of the issue involving all levels of managers and employees. There needs to be widespread understanding and acceptance of the need for profit as an integral part of nonprofit corporate financial health. There need not be great tension around fiscal decisions regarding profit if the realities of nonprofit finance are understood by all key players.

Why Capitalization Is Not a Four-Letter Word

O   ur candidate for the most underappreciated (pun intended) area of nonprofit financial management is capitalization. Nonprofit managers historically have paid scant attention to this aspect of their operations. For one thing, most nonprofit organizations don't do things that require capital expenditures—or at least they don't think they do. For another, only the larger nonprofits such as universities and hospitals have access to the bond markets, which is what typically prompts serious attention to capital structure. Finally, some percentage of nonprofit managers share a frequently unspoken discomfort with the whole idea of capitalism or anything that smacks of it.

Ironically, next to maintaining cash flow and profitability, using the capital entrusted to it is perhaps the most important financial choice a nonprofit organization will make. To a degree that varies with the services the organization provides, one use of capital is to acquire assets such as property, plant and equipment. Analyzing that choice turns out to be easy.

THE ANALYSIS AND HOW IT WORKS

We'll go right to the punch line and work backwards from there. Your de facto policy toward capital asset acquisition and management is called the accounting age of property, plant and equipment, and it can be inferred from your most recent IRS Form 990. Find line 57c, accumulated depreciation, on the form and divide it by line 42,

Column A, depreciation expense. The resulting number tells you a lot about your capital asset management policies. The higher the number, the older your property. The lower the number, the more up-to-date your investment.

Although nominally measured in years, this number is really an index, a pure number whose greatest usefulness is its size (as well as the way it compares with the same index from other comparable groups—more on that later). Here's why.

When you purchase a capital asset—normally considered to be a thing of value that will last well over 12 months such as a piece of real estate, a large item such as a computer, or a motor vehicle—the asset goes down in your financial records at the cost of its acquisition. So a building that cost $100,000 will show up on the balance sheet as an asset worth that amount (although it will usually be grouped with similar assets, so it may not be possible to identify that asset separately). Note that it doesn't make any difference in this area how the asset purchase was financed; only the purchase price is important. For financial purposes, assets are regarded as having a limited life span. This is known as the useful life of the asset. Furthermore, each year the owner is considered to "use up" a portion of that asset. This is called depreciation.

Almost always in the nonprofit sector, depreciation is calculated by dividing the cost of the asset by its useful life. If that $100,000 asset had a useful life of 10 years—useful lives are usually established by convention—then depreciation is considered to be $100,000/10, or $10,000 per year. Each year the organization must show $10,000 as an expense of doing business.

If a nonprofit only owned one piece of capital equipment, keeping track of depreciation would be a cinch. But assets are acquired every year, and after a while old assets are fully depreciated, which means that they no longer show up on the balance sheet. Plus, virtually every active asset originally cost a different amount and is at a different point in its useful life. The result is that each asset must be tracked separately and the totals lumped together to create an overall total for the year. This is what is meant by the schedule of depreciation.

Adding the total amount of depreciation registered by all active assets gives the agency's total depreciation expense for that year, and that's what is shown in line 42 of the 990. Adding together the total amount of depreciation charged to date against each individual asset since it was first acquired gives the accumulated depreciation shown in line 57b. Dividing line 57c by line 42a gives the accounting age of property, plant and equipment.

WHAT IT MEANS

This is more than an exercise in division. The accounting age of property, plant and equipment is effectively a guide to the time frame by which the organization is managed. One of the first places that financially pressed managers often cut is capital expenditures—putting off that renovation, buying one vehicle when two are really needed, and so on. Capital expenditures are "big ticket" items so they are a natural target of budget cutters, but, perhaps more important, the effect of going without a needed asset can be subtle and take a few years to show up.

Hospitals, for example, must make routinely large investments in buildings and equipment in order to attract and hold physicians who make referrals. In turn, those referrals generate revenue which generates profits that allow further capital investment to attract and hold physicians, etc. Stretching the investment cycle in the name of saving money (i.e., letting the accounting age of property, plant and equipment drift upward) can mean the beginning of gradual decline for the organization.

Many other types of organizations will find this measure useful as well. Groups who provide residential care and who purchase their own facilities will find the ratio extremely helpful in monitoring their performance. In these cases the absence of a meaningful ratio will be equally significant, since a residential care provider that rents every single one of its buildings necessarily has a dramatically shortened time horizon for its programming—the end of its leasing period.

What should the ratio be? There is no universally applicable answer to this question, but lower is obviously better ("younger"). For nonprofits whose assets are largely computers and office equipment, the number should probably be no higher than five to seven. If buildings are owned, and they tend to be located in older urban areas, add a year or two to those numbers. A ratio in the double digits should be considered a red flag under most circumstances.

"BUT WE DON'T OWN ANYTHING"

With proper care and analysis this test can be applied to organizations that own no real estate and don't need to invest in expensive specialized equipment. Why? Because almost every organization today needs to make regular investments in computer equipment. Considering that information technology usually has a useful life of three to five years, if computers were the only significant type of capital asset that an agency were to buy, an accounting age of more than five years would suggest that the organization is falling behind in its information processing capability. A quick walk around the office would probably confirm that hypothesis.

Finally, the accounting age ratio is ideally suited to comparisons with comparable organizations, or benchmarking. Knowing others' results can be an invaluable guide to planning since the simple mathematics of accounting age ratios means that they will tend to change gradually over time rather than abruptly. Knowing benchmarks also helps put an individual agency's results into context. National and statewide associations are often good sources of benchmarks, as are consultants and researchers.

The Formula

To calculate your accounting age of property, plant and equipment use the following formula:

$$\frac{\text{Accumulated Depreciation (Line 57c)}}{\text{Depreciation (Line 42a)}}$$

The answer is expressed as a number of years—7.2 years, 9.0 years, etc. Being an average, this does not mean that every asset owned by the organization is 7.2 years old. The mixture of assets owned is an important variable. The more the mixture is weighted toward bigger, longer-term assets the higher the number will be. For nonprofits with only office furniture and miscellaneous equipment as capital assets the number should be in the low single digit range.

In Cash There Is Opportunity

For nonprofit organizations, cash is power. The nonprofit that has cash is well positioned to seize opportunities and cope with crises. The organization with no cash, staggers. Historically, nonprofit organizations seem to expect to have little cash. In fact, the symptoms of cash strain define a part of nonprofits' collective self-image: missed and nearly missed payrolls, frantic grant applications to head off a cash crisis, a pervasive sense of going without.

There are many reasons for this state of affairs, and they range from extremely valid to the merely habitual. But the one thing they all have in common is that they are the result of ideas—our own ideas about how nonprofits should be managed, funding sources' ideas about financial policies, and boards of directors' ideas about priorities. So the first step in changing these common results is changing the ideas that permit them to happen.

This is a story about how one nonprofit organization, Sunnyvale Elder Services (SES), improved its cash flow fairly dramatically over a five-year period. The story is a mixture of familiar elements: hard work, planning, careful personnel selection, and just plain good luck. Most of the elements of SES' success can be copied by others, in one way or another.

In 1989, SES experienced a bad year. This elder service provider with revenues of $5 million suffered a $194,000 loss, and its days' cash ratio was a mere 14 days. The organization's books and records were in disarray and the June 30 fiscal year-end was not officially closed for seven months. Shortly thereafter, the chief financial officer (CFO) abruptly resigned. Meanwhile, the agency's chief funding

Measuring Cash Flow

Many aspects of nonprofit management are hard to measure. Cash flow, fortunately, is not one of them. There are many measures of liquidity, but the one we will use is the days' cash ratio. In its simplest form, the days' cash ratio offers an answer to a hypothetically bleak question. If all incoming cash was completely shut off and yet the organization continued to spend at its normal daily average rate, how long would the corporation survive?

Already you can see the purely hypothetical nature of this measurement. No organization's incoming cash is ever likely to be completely shut off, and if it were, only a fool would continue spending at the previous daily average rate. Nevertheless, because everyone shares the same assumptions in calculating the days' cash ratio it is a useful way to measure cash flow.

For the mathematically inclined, the formula for days' cash is:

$$\frac{(\text{Total yearly expenses} - \text{Depreciation})}{365} = X$$

$$\frac{\text{Total Cash}}{X} = \text{Days' cash}$$

Or, to express the same formula in terms of the appropriate line items on the IRS Form 990 that nonprofits complete each year:

$$\frac{\#17 - \#42}{365} = X$$

$$\frac{(\#45 + \#46)}{X} = X$$

Note that we subtracted depreciation from total yearly expenses before calculating the daily average spending. Depreciation is not a cash expense, and we are only concerned about expenses that have to be covered by writing a check.

Table 5.   Measuring Cash Flow

Many aspects of nonprofit management are hard to measure. Cash flow, fortunately, is not one of them. There are many measures of liquidity, but the one we will use is the days' cash ratio. In its simplest form, the days cash ratio offers an answer to a hypothetically bleak question: If all incoming cash was completely shut off and yet the organization continued to spend at its normal daily average rate, how long would the corporation survive?

Already you can see the purely hypothetical nature of this measurement. No organization's incoming cash is ever likely to be completely shut off, and if it were only a fool would continue spending at the previous daily average rate. Nevertheless, because everyone shares the same assumptions in calculating the day's cash ratio it is a useful way to measure cash flow.

For the mathematically inclined, the formula for days' cash is:

$$\frac{\text{(Total yearly expenses} - \text{Depreciation)}}{365} = X$$

$$\frac{\text{Total Cash}}{X} = \text{Days' cash}$$

Or, to express the same formula in terms of the appropriate line items on the IRS Form 990 that nonprofits complete each year:

$$\frac{\text{Line \#17} - \text{Line \#42}}{365} = X \qquad \frac{\text{Line \#45} + \text{Line \#46}}{X} = X$$

Note that we subtracted depreciation from total yearly expenses before calculating the daily average spending. Depreciation is not a cash expense, and we are only concerned about expenses that have to be covered by writing a check.

---

source, state government, was expressing open dissatisfaction with its financial performance.

End of bad news. Starting from that low point, the organization took a series of steps that produced almost immediate payoffs. Measures of its success can be found in Table 5. Note the steady increase in days' cash. It is not a coincidence that SES' profitability has also steadily improved. SES' turnaround can be attributed to a number of factors. Here are some of the important ones:

Hired a qualified CFO. The new CFO had received academic training in accounting and MIS and spent the two previous years working in a similar organization. He understood the special nature of nonprofit accounting and finance and was committed to the field. A qualified CFO for a nonprofit organization is really the product of a number of factors. Obviously, academic training in accounting— or solid, extensive, and verifiable experience in the field—is a must.

Beyond technical qualifications, intangibles are perhaps most important. Can they communicate fiscal information and policies to all of their staff? Do they understand the role of a nonprofit? Most important, are they a leader?

Note that the term "CFO" may be misleading, or it may have connotations of something only very large corporations can afford. The point here is that any nonprofit, no matter how large or small, needs to identify at least one person as primarily responsible for financial matters. The level of training and experience can and should vary according to a wide number of factors, but ultimately the responsibility is the same regardless of the size of the organization.

Took advantage of speeded-up reimbursement. Most governmental contractual relationships, especially in this field, involve significant delays in payment. SES' state government funder recognized that starving its service providers for cash ultimately weakens the services they are contracted to provide. Their alternative system of payments allows providers to receive automatically up to 1/24th of the yearly contract amount at the middle and end of each month, with each end of the month payment being reconciled up or down to reflect fluctuations in utilization.

Planned cash flow. The CFO and his assistant began by doing regular cash flow planning. Starting with the existing cash balance, they would determine how much cash could reasonably be expected over the next few days or weeks and then compare that with how much cash they anticipated having to spend. That way, they were able to determine well in advance when their "crisis periods" would probably occur. Now that the procedure is down to a science, they need only a few minutes to estimate what cash inflow and outflow can be expected over the next day or two—or over the next several months.

More important, SES now has sizable cash balances, and management has worked with their bank to develop conservative temporary investment plans. This step alone can mean thousands of dollars in additional yearly interest income when dealing with SES' volume of cash on hand.

Stretched payables. Inexplicably, some nonprofits struggle with cash flow while paying their bills within days of receipt. SES schedules payables for action according to the vendor's expectations for payment. If the vendor expects payment within 45 days, they get paid within about 40 days. On the other hand, if a vendor offers a discount for payment within a certain period of time, SES takes it. The CFO has even initiated negotiations with some vendors to offer discounts, thereby using the agency's good cash flow to lower operating costs.

Stretching payables is a perfectly valid cash flow strategy, but it obviously requires the nonprofit to work closely with its vendors. As the CFO says, "they have to be happy and we have to be happy, otherwise it doesn't work."

Turned a yearly profit. Profitability is the nonprofit manager's most reliable source of cash. Unfortunately, there are a lot of myths and misconceptions around the notion of profit in a nonprofit, so it takes leadership and confidence for an organization to use this strategy. But that's material for another story. Or maybe five more stories.

The question can now be fairly asked: So what? SES is sitting on a mound of cash, the financial staff is disciplined to keep it that way, and a healthy little supply of economic resources has been captured by a single nonprofit. What has really been accomplished?

The answer is that SES is now positioned to do two things: weather crises and seize opportunities. If revenue begins to decline due to changes in funder policies, SES' elder clients have some measure of temporary insulation from the effects. No organization strapped for cash can hope to serve as a temporary buffer for its users.

SES can also invest in its own operations to support its overall strategic direction. For example, most serious analysts of elder services agree that case management will be an essential component of service in the future. Underlying any case management system is a good computerized information system. SES is now well positioned to upgrade its hardware and software investment to support its ability to provide case management. Note also that such an investment, in accounting terms, would not immediately be an expense of operations but simply a change in the way assets are held, from cash to equipment. In short, SES has created opportunities for itself and its service users.

The cash flow issues facing SES are the same as those facing most nonprofits in this country. This particular mix of tactics and strategies may not be applicable, as a package, to every nonprofit, but the general themes of their success are quite relevant. A nonprofit's cash flow is very manageable—with the right tools.

Indirect Secrets, or Why Nonprofits Will Never Have $80 Screwdrivers

Recently we had conversations with two different nonprofit managers, each of whom was quite pleased that their organizations routinely post administrative costs of close to 8 percent. "We try to put the money into direct care," said one.

A laudable though completely predictable sentiment. Is there any nonprofit manager out there whose agency tries to spend money on overhead expenses instead of direct service?

Like most such assertions, this one was as much an expression of philosophy as a statement of fact. From what we knew of both agencies, they certainly did not overspend on administrative costs. On the other hand, they were not cold water bathrooms, 60 watt-bulbs, and reuse-the-teabag-types either.

Ironically, just a few miles away from where one of the executive directors sat was a major research-intensive university that we happen to know carries a routine overhead rate of over 100 percent. And while we have never asked, we suspect that that organization would also say it likes to keep its overhead low and put most of its funds directly into education.

How can one explain this seeming paradox? Is it really true that two nonprofits can have such dramatically different overhead rates? Who's mistaken here?

DEFINING AND CALCULATING INDIRECT COSTS

The puzzling answer is that there is no mistake. They're both right, each in their own way. For its part, the vast majority of the university's buildings are relatively no more opulent than those of the smaller nonprofit. And although the university does generally have a much larger overhead structure, it's certainly not 12.5 times larger, as its 100 percent overhead rate would suggest. So why are they both right?

The answer begins with the definition of the term *indirect cost* (we'll use the term indirect cost, although it can be called other things as well, such as administrative cost, management expense, general and administrative expense, overhead, etc.). Costs clearly associated with the mission of a nonprofit such as full-time staff who work in programs and the cost of supplies that the programs use are easily attributed to programs in most accounting systems. This means that they are direct costs.

Many kinds of costs, however, cannot reasonably be attributed directly. These include things like the bookkeeper's time, the cost of the agency sign in front of the building, and the replacement cartridges for the laser printers. The key word here is reasonable. Given enough time, a large enough computer, a fantastically detailed accounting system, and an army of analysts one could probably turn every single indirect cost into a direct cost. But that would be onerous and pointless, so the conventional answer is to create a category for indirect costs.

The next challenge is to calculate it. Table 6 shows a highly sim-

Table 6.   Agency Budget

Item	Dollars
Executive Director	$60,000
Program Managers (2)	80,000
Administrative Assistant (1)	25,000
Direct Service Staff	200,000
Payroll Taxes & Benefits (22% of salaries)	80,300
Direct Supplies	40,000
Program Rent	10,000
Administrative Rent	5,000
Vehicle Costs	5,000
Miscellaneous	2,000
TOTAL	$507,300

plified nonprofit agency budget based on a two-program agency and various related expenses. What is the agency's indirect cost rate? If you said 10 percent you'd be right. If you said 71 percent you'd also be right. And if you gave a variety of other percentages you'd probably be right as well, *because it all depends on how you define indirect costs.*

Here's how we get those two very different results. In Table 7, we try to make every conceivable expense a direct charge. So we argue that the executive director, normally an indirect cost, spends fully half of her time supervising the two program directors. The administrative assistant is said to spend a third of her time dealing with indirect matters, and we accept the full charge for rental of the administrative space.

In Table 8, we define indirect expenses extremely broadly. This is what happens in federal funding (like what our university gets), where recipient organizations must charge a federal overhead rate based on a specific formula. This is why the Pentagon is often accused of buying $80 screwdrivers (for example, $4.00 for the screwdriver and a

Table 7. Aggressive Computation of Indirect Costs (10%)

Item	Dollars
Executive Director	$60,000
Program Managers (2)	80,000
Administrative Assistant (1)	25,000
Direct Service Staff	200,000
Payroll Taxes & Benefits (22% of salaries)	80,300
Direct Supplies	40,000
Program Rent	10,000
Administrative Rent	5,000
Vehicle Costs	5,000
Miscellaneous	2,000
TOTAL	$507,300

Formula: Indirect costs are drawn from the shaded areas. Based on this example, that means:

• 50% of the Executive Director's time plus 22% for taxes and benefits for a total of $36,600

• 33% of the Administrative Assistant's time plus 22% for taxes and benefits for a total of $10,065

• $5,000 for administrative rent

This produces a total indirect cost of $51,665. This indirect cost as a percentage of total cost creates an indirect rate of 10%.

Table 8.   Broad Computation of Indirect Cost (71%)

Item	Dollars
Executive Director	$60,000
Program Managers (2)	80,000
Administrative Assistant (1)	25,000
Direct Service Staff	200,000
Payroll Taxes & Benefits (22% of salaries)	80,300
Direct Supplies	40,000
Program Rent	10,000
Administrative Rent	5,000
Vehicle Costs	5,000
Miscellaneous	2,000
TOTAL	$507,300

Formula: Indirect costs are again drawn from the shaded areas. Indirect costs are:

• 100% of the time of all staff other than direct service staff plus 22% for taxes and benefits for a total of $201,300

• 100% of administrative rent and vehicle costs $10,000

This totals $211,300, making the indirect rate 71%. Remember, unlike in the previous example, we're defining indirect cost as a percentage of direct costs, not total budget. Direct cost is $296,000, so $211,300/296,000 is 71%.

$76.00 automatic overhead charge on every order). In this computation we also express the rate as a percentage of direct costs, not on the total budget as in the first example, which drives the rate even higher.

WHY IT MATTERS

All of this seemingly obscure technical calculation is important for two reasons. First, the general public believes that indirect costs in a nonprofit are inherently bad and should be minimized or eliminated altogether. Although we in the nonprofit management sector may know better, we have to go along or risk losing funding or credibility. So we attempt to creatively define indirect costs out of existence.

But the real problem is that, by claiming our indirect rates are rock-bottom low, we are subtly devaluing the work of management. That will be an even bigger problem in the future because the demands of the external environment are forcing the cost of management up, not down. Greater use of technology, the need to do more fundraising, and the overall cost of doing business all drive indirect costs up. Those who believe they can get away with less and less spending in this area are simply being shortsighted.

Yet the tension will continue. The average donor, empowered with more and more freely available information about nonprofit recipients, will demand low indirect costs as a condition of philanthropy. Media outlets are becoming savvier about the implied cost-benefit ratio of indirect costs to direct costs.

The pressure to report low indirect costs will not go away. Considering the relative lack of other structural pressures on nonprofits, this may very well be healthy for the sector overall. But that doesn't mean individual nonprofit managers should take their own press releases too literally. They must find a way to honestly report competitively low indirect costs even as they pay more and more attention to management matters. That can be our little secret.

Critical Juncture Financing

Here's the problem. Nonprofit organizations in this country are at the very beginning of a massive stage of restructuring driven by a variety of factors both positive and negative. That restructuring can lead to things as diverse as alliances, mergers, joint ventures, shared activities, bankruptcy, or voluntary termination. Individual nonprofits reach this kind of critical juncture in different ways and at their own pace, but what most have in common is that they did not plan for the associated costs. Some may even find that the major barrier they face is not a lack of will or desire, but a lack of financing for their chosen path.

Whether that critical juncture is reached through strength or crisis, most nonprofits find that there are few templates to guide them. Therefore, the foundations that fund them and other potential resource providers must grope through the process without tools or widely accepted models for assistance. All parties drift, improvise, and hope for the best. What is needed now is a way for funders to offer concrete, specific assistance, and shared models for encouraging productive, collaborative strategies.

CRITICAL JUNCTURE FINANCING (CJF)

Here's a solution: Critical Juncture Financing, or CJF.

CJF could become a way for foundations and other interested funders to encourage joint action and creative restructuring in the service of their missions. Modified from an idea first suggested by the staff at Philadelphia Health Care Management Corporation, CJF would be *any kind of financial resource provided by a third party which is intended to facilitate the successful transition of two or more nonprofit organizations to the next stage of their development.*

A few points about this concept. First, the key in the above definition is that the juncture must involve two or more organizations, for reasons that will be explained later. Troubled agencies need partners, and successful organizations can draw strength from well-designed collaborations. Second, we are talking about resources that finance a transition, not just conventional grants for programming. Finally, the definition specifically mentions third parties, which can be virtually any type of organization such as foundations, associations, related corporations, lenders, and even other nonprofits.

WHAT SHOULD CJF BE USED FOR?

Exactly what should Critical Juncture Financing be used for? The short answer is that it should finance common nonprofit management activities undertaken by two or more nonprofits.

For example, simply closing down a nonprofit corporation takes resources. Often, a nonprofit that wants to close its doors cannot do so because it can't raise money to pay for the assistance it needs to close down. CJF would remedy this problem—but only if the termination directly involves another nonprofit public charity. There are usually state laws involving just such a situation, of course, but the spirit of CJF is such that it should be compatible with any state's charity termination regulations.

CJF could also pay for the costs associated with mergers of two or more nonprofits. This would include legal and financial advisors as well as consultants. It may also cover one-time costs such as lease buyouts or moving expenses. Similarly, CJF might be used to cover some of the start-up costs associated with an alliance. This could range from consultant fees to staff support to one-time capital investments.

A good way to use CJF funding would be to leverage investments in information technology. Many nonprofits need to upgrade their computer systems and are beginning to seek other nonprofit partners to share the costs of doing so. Adding a bit of CJF funding could make the difference between a short-term fix and a truly long-term information management solution that neither party could afford alone.

Some nonprofits are considering ways to consolidate their administrative and financial systems. These "backroom" functions could often be performed by larger units with more sophisticated systems and capabilities but, again, it takes capital investment and start-up cash flow to get there. CJF could help here too.

As a prelude to more formal collaborations, two or more nonprofits might explore shared management positions—a chief financial officer, a human resource person, development professional, etc. CJF might be used temporarily for this purpose, or it might help defray part of the costs for an extended start-up period.

WHAT IT IS, WHAT IT ISN'T

CJF could take many forms. The obvious one is a traditional grant from a grantmaking organization. But it could also be a loan, akin to either a start-up investment in a for-profit company or to standard equipment or cash flow loans. More innovative would be forgiveness of outstanding debts so as to free up cash or borrowing power. A more conventional approach would be the provision of in-kind services to two or more nonprofits going through a shared critical juncture.

As important as what CJF is, there are many things it should *not* be. It should not be financing targeted at a single nonprofit: leave that for conventional vehicles. It should never fund bad debts, deferred compensation, single-owner assets, simple program expansion, or ordinary strategic planning (unless it is done jointly). Nor should it be entirely free. We tend not to value that which comes at no cost. CJF should be intended as leverage financing that, when combined with resources supplied by the participants, creates a full package of resources necessary to accomplish a collaborative purpose.

Just as important is the question of who should supply CJF. Clearly, traditional foundations are in the best position to provide critical juncture financing. They already deal with potential recipients, they understand the sector, they have a sense of which proposals will and won't work. Their infrastructure and funding models could easily expand to include the concept of CJF.

But CJF could also be provided by associations and others outside the immediate orbit of service provision and traditional funding. The national offices of large national organizations are already beginning to experiment with a de facto equivalent of CJF as they work with affiliates to restructure and refocus their activities. Even trade associations and advocacy groups could provide a version of CJF under the right circumstances. Banks may consider a focused version such as loan forgiveness in return for a collaborative solution to certain clients' long-standing financial problems. Individual donors are ideally suited for making CJF investments as an almost surefire way of affecting their favorite organizations, although admittedly it may be a difficult message to get across to nonprofessionals.

CJF is neither a service nor a patented product. It is purely a concept, and if it is to have any impact it must be widely discussed and adopted. So if it sounds like something worth doing, spread the word. The next organization to benefit from it could be yours—which means it will help the whole sector.

Where to Find Cost Savings

A vignette that's not as petty as it seems:

> *We were conducting an operations review of a nonprofit nursing home, examining all aspects of administrative and financial management policies and procedures. In the course of the review, we learned that the evening nurses on the second floor were ordering presharpened pencils when everyone else in the facility seemed to be content with the old-fashioned, sharpen-it-yourself kind. Annual cost of this practice: about $35.*

A second vignette that's just about as significant as it seems:

> *As a board member, we recently sat through an extended discussion about the agency's mental health clinic. The program was only getting paid about seventy percent of its actual costs and the resulting deficit was hurting the other programs. Board members tried to be helpful. Have you cut back on all unnecessary spending? Yes. Have you tried to better match therapists' availability with scheduled hours? Yes, but we can't do much better without an expensive scheduling system. Have you reduced management hours? Yes. And so on.*

What do these two vignettes have in common? They each illustrate a simple but profound truth about nonprofit management: Real cost savings are produced by focusing on systems, not transactions.

A CLOSER LOOK

Let's look at how this maxim applies to the pencil caper. This simple situation illustrates many things. Some of them are trivial, like the fact that this particular group of people apparently preferred to write with very sharp pencils that someone else sharpens. Who doesn't?

Dig a bit deeper for some thought-provoking insights. For starters, why do nurses have to take valuable time away from their clinical duties to order pencils? Every minute spent fumbling for the stationery supplies order form is a minute taken away from the residents. If they must get involved at this level, imagine how much time they must be spending on other unproductive activities.

Second, why do second shift nurses have the authority to order supplies at all? A little investigation revealed that they were never even told that they had to order their supplies from the same vendor as the other floors, so it was at least theoretically possible that the facility could have as many different stationery supply vendors as they had people ordering supplies.

Finally, what was it about this group of nurses that caused them to need so many pencils in the first place? Other shifts on other floors showed a marked preference for pens rather than pencils. Was it something they were doing right? Or wrong?

Needless to say, the administrative and financial systems in the nursing home were weak and near collapse. There was no leadership, no clarity about roles, and no sense of teamwork. It was this lack of systems that created the nursing home's true problems, *not* the purchasing of presharpened pencils. The solution was agency-wide systems for centralized purchasing, budgeting, and clinical quality assurance.

In many ways, the mental health clinic is the complete reverse of the nursing home. Whereas the nursing home was acting as a buyer without systems to manage its purchasing, the mental health clinic was acting as supplier to a highly sophisticated buyer known as a managed care system.

Although the clinic's situation is considerably more complex, we can reasonably infer one of two things. One interpretation is that the clinic is a notably inefficient supplier of services in an environment where everyone else has figured out how to provide similar services for less money. Another interpretation is that the clinic is no better or worse than any other and that its buyers have simply figured out how to buy mental health services for less money.

It turns out that this clinic is run by smart, competent people. If there are reasonable cost savings to be had, they have probably already taken them. That suggests that the second interpretation—that the managed care folks are willfully paying below market prices because they know they can get away with it—is the correct one.

The real question for the clinic is how long they can (or want to) go along like this. Either they are going to have to massively restructure the way they provide services and hope that they can then break even as a result, or they are going to have to put their faith in external forces to somehow change the managed care environment.

IT'S IN THE SYSTEM

The common point here is that both the nursing home and the clinic have problems rooted in systems, and that the solutions to their problems will also have to be systemic. It makes no sense to hassle the second shift nurses for their pencil transactions because it's the underlying systems that need the attention. And the clinic has such fundamental problems that it cannot expect them to be solved just by tweaking the specifics of a few transactions.

As the demands of managed care and other cost-related pressures on nonprofits increase, more and more nonprofits find themselves looking for cost savings. If you find yourself needing some cost savings for your organization, here are a few things to keep in mind:

Be clear about your twin roles as seller and buyer. Every nonprofit is a seller in that it offers services in return for revenue. Every nonprofit is also a buyer when it buys staff time, supplies, occupancy services, and the like. Is the pressure for cost savings coming from your role as seller or buyer or both? Another way of saying this is that cost savings must be found to cope with too little revenue (seller) or too many expenses (buyer). Different sources of pressure dictate different coping strategies.

Start with transactions. Without question, begin by looking at specific transactions. This may sound like a contradiction after the above material, but transactions are the things most readily visible to managers. They float on the surface of the organization, as it were, and they offer the only real pathways into the logic of the underlying systems. Treat each transaction as holding a potential clue to those underlying systems, much as the pencils did for the nursing home.

Move quickly to systems. Evaluate transactions by clustering them according to commonalties. These may include things such as common employees, similar processes, and shared products. Once you group them, use the 80/20 rule to focus on the important ones first—that is, 80 percent of the benefit will be gained from working on 20 percent of the transactions. Go for the transaction themes that offer the highest leverage. The clinic's analysis was ready-made—all of the troubled transactions involved third party managed care organizations. Other situations are not so obvious.

Keep sight of the big picture. It is quite easy to feel busy and virtuous when trying to find savings, but it will count for nothing if the larger context is structurally hostile. This is what is happening with the mental health clinic. Rhetoric aside, the managed care organizations simply may not want all clinics to succeed, and they may be using a period of transition rates to weed out the smaller, weaker players. If so, no amount of hard work will help, and the agency will eventually have to stop providing that service. Acknowledging that possibility is difficult, but this is the time to start.

Few nonprofits ever succeeded on the strength of cost saving zeal alone. But when it is necessary, managers will concentrate on systems rather than transactions. Finding savings is more than just a matter of not sharpening the pencils.

Recovering from a Case of Parentheses

Take out your most recent audited balance sheet. Find the liabilities section and look for the term *net assets*. Look to the right of that term. Do you see parentheses? If you do, get a glass of water and sit down. Relax. Read this section thoroughly. It is a quick financial survival kit, and it could save your agency.

If you are like many nonprofit managers and board members you won't see parentheses, though you may see a number perilously close to zero. If the latter is true—or if the number next to that term has been declining steadily over the years—get that glass of water. If the number is big and healthy and has been that way for some time, read the chapter anyway. You could be in parentheses yourself someday.

What you have just done is one of the quickest possible tests for financial solvency, and it is one test that an increasing number of nonprofits are having trouble passing. Net assets is the term describing the cumulative financial value of the nonprofit corporation. The term used to be known as fund balance until fairly recently when the accounting profession decided to make it more precise. For-profit firms call it a number of things such as net worth, owners' equity, retained earnings, shareholders' equity, etc.

Whatever it's called, it grows the same way: by adding each year's profit. It also gets reduced by every deficit (special adjustments having nothing to do with yearly profits or losses can change it as well). So the number is a kind of running report card on both management's decisions and funding sources' policies.

If the net assets number is in parentheses the organization has no cumulative net worth. What that means is that, all things being equal, if the agency were to close down as of that day and sell its assets to pay off its liabilities—assuming the assets fetched prices close to the value the books showed they had—then the agency would be unable to make good on at least some of its liabilities. This state of affairs is better known as bankruptcy.

If you discover parentheses where you'd rather see none—or if you discover a pattern of declining net assets linked to routine operating losses—there are a few things you should do:

1. Take it seriously. Hard as it is to believe, many nonprofit managers and their boards of directors don't take this situation seriously. Or, to be precise, they say that they take it seriously but don't follow up with any action. So an executive director or his/her board worries about the negative net assets but discounts it with a comforting or dismissive explanation. Some examples:

- "It was a smaller negative net assets figure than we thought it would be."
- "It has only been three bad years out of thirty."
- "Most of the loss was due to depreciation."
- "Everyone is feeling the same pinch."

Most of these responses are irrelevant or misinformed and serve mainly to excuse inaction. Unfortunately, when a great many people in a nonprofit's leadership positions do not appreciate how desperate their financial picture truly is, these responses are likely to go unchallenged. Note that there are a few unique situations, rooted in accounting policies, in which the reality of an agency's financial picture is much brighter than the records show. For example, a major asset carried by the corporation may be fully depreciated but have a high market value which does not show up on the balance sheet. These types of situations are rare, however, and for the most part one must assume that the financial reporting is faithful to reality.

2. Stop the hemorrhaging immediately. If the net assets are negative, they got that way via a steady stream of losses each year. Chances are, those losses are continuing. They must be stopped—*now*. In all probability this means that the agency must spend less money than it has been spending, since revenues are hard to boost on short notice and since prior managers have probably already explored these options. Consequently management must make cuts in current spending levels, and the sooner the better.

3. Don't just talk about it, make a plan. A small group of managers, including board members if appropriate, should devise a solution to the problem. The priorities here are to make the plan realistic and to put it together quickly—a sizable negative net asset problem will usually get worse as time goes on. Timeliness is more important than elegance and articulate documentation. Nor does the plan have to be comprehensive, at least in the beginning. It can be buffed up later—the spirit should be *"ready, fire, aim."*

4. Pull a financial fire alarm. The whole agency needs confirmation of the problem and some indication that you're attempting to make it right. Notice we say *confirmation of the problem*—it's very hard to hide financial difficulty. Staff members will suspect what's going on even if it's never confirmed. Announcing the existence of the problem accomplishes two things. First, it gets the problem out into the open where it can be handled better. Second, if dealt with properly, it can be part of the solution. Finally, it buys a little time.

This is where your plan gets used. Announcing financial difficulty alone is a little like staff abuse. Staff may think that somehow or other, management must have created the problem so it should be up to management to solve it. Just announcing fiscal trouble and then walking away can damage staff morale, public image, and even continued funding. Worse, it can be counterproductive, creating resentment and fear.

But giving the bad news accompanied by a plausible recovery plan and a request for staff feedback and additional ideas can turn a negative story into a positive one of motivation and trust. By inviting staff participation in crafting an agencywide response, management creates a single focus point for action. Just as important, it communicates respect for others' ideas. And the feedback and ideas should be sought aggressively and in person, not just by saying "the door is always open." Not coincidentally, this approach also lifts a bit of the onus for a solution from management.

5. Monitor the response. This is where most agencies fall down. The recovery plan may go through several different versions, but the final provisions need to be monitored for effectiveness. It is entirely possible that some of the initial financial problems were caused by inattentiveness, so this step may be particularly difficult to continue over time. It is also likely that the shortcomings of the current financial reporting system will be highlighted during this period. Take notes: if the plan works, you'll get a chance to fix the reporting system later.

If the plan doesn't work, it is time to consider a different approach. The obvious one is a merger with a financially stronger agency. The problem is that at this point there may not be much value left in the organization to attract a merger partner. The best time to merge is when a nonprofit doesn't face a financial crisis, and if the crisis has already defeated one effort at resolution there is even less reason to think that another attempt will succeed.

The best approach is always preventive. Protect your assets, minimize your liabilities, maintain program quality. And keep your eye out for parentheses.

Soliciting Mistrust

Dinner is done and the kids have finished their baths and are climbing into bed when the phone rings.

"Hi, this is Jim Morgan of the Blankville Fire Department. How are you this evening?"

"Fine," we say. "How are you?"

"Well, I can't complain, and when I do, no one listens," he chuckles. "You know . . . working the evening shift here and all."

We knew what he meant. We worked the evening shift once. It can be very lonely. We have a mental image of this stoic public servant squeezing civic-minded calls in between fire alarms. What follows is a blur of words. Special fundraising appeal . . . Red Sox and Celtics . . . tickets donated . . . program book . . . donation. As he wraps up, a question comes to mind. "Jim, are you a Blankville firefighter?" He seems surprised by the question. "Well . . . no, actually I work with them . . . for a company . . ."

"Jim, thanks for calling."

There are a handful of ways for nonprofit organizations to raise money. Using volunteer help is an obvious and widely successful method for many. Large and well established charities such as universities, hospitals, and some cultural organizations typically have fundraising professionals on their staff. There are also fundraising consultants who work with any size organization to research, design, or carry out specific fundraising projects. What all of these methods have in common is that the individual or organization is involved only in seeking funds, never in actually handling the money raised. The problem areas tend to be with the professional solicitors who both seek funds and handle the money that comes in, giving the designated charity a percentage of the amount raised.

Because these kinds of solicitors effectively work on commission, the potential for abuse is large. The worst kind of professional solicitor is an efficient, cynical operation. These companies use sophisticated telephone lists and demographic information, often computerized. They talk of their intended targets as "grapes," and they speak of a successful donation as "making a hit." The names of their charities are frequently deliberately similar to well-known organizations or contain buzz words such as "conservation" or "public safety." They often link their fundraising appeals to mops, brooms, sports tickets, flags, ads in program books, and the like.

Small businesses are flooded with their calls, but many also go straight to the home where they can be especially persistent. What keeps these organizations in business is a kind of three-way gridlock of economic interests and legal rulings. With relatively little capital investment required and a more or less immediate cash flow possible, it's an easy business to enter. For the charities' part, even a low percentage of the overall take can be better than nothing, so anything produced by the companies seems like found money. Often the charities involved—when they are bona fide organizations and not just fronts for the companies—are small local affairs with neither the interest nor the ability to mount an in-house fundraising effort.

The third leg of the gridlock is the legal and regulatory environment, which has changed recently. A while ago, there was a legal cap of 25 percent on the amount that professional fundraisers could charge after expenses. When that provision was struck down as unconstitutional, regulators started seeing contracts between charities and solicitation companies that were "awful" in the words of one regulator. Although companies must often post bonds and the charities themselves may be required to report on their fundraising expenditures, the existing set of laws and regulations provides limited tools with which to pursue unethical or illegal solicitations.

The irony is that most of these problems would evaporate if consumers held their charitable transactions to the same standards as a commercial product or service, yet doing so feels like it tarnishes the action. The act of donating to a public charity carries with it a great deal of trust and free will. Intimidation or cynical manipulation cheapen the process. And that is perhaps the real offense of unethical solicitation. As traditional government funding of many nonprofit charities declines, they will turn increasingly to a public that is being conned. What's being stolen is not just money, but trust.

How to Transfer a Few Trillion Dollars

Fortune magazine started it all a few years ago with an estimate of $8 trillion. Cornell University economist Robert Avery then pegged it at $5 trillion. Others such as Ann Kaplan of the American Association of Fundraising Council Trust for Philanthropy said it could go as high as $10 trillion. Now estimates are coming in at ten and fifteen times that number. Whatever the source or the estimate, it is abundantly clear that we are at the beginning stages of the greatest intergenerational transfer of wealth ever witnessed in this country.

The population of millionaires in this country is aging. The average millionaire just a few years ago was 57. The average millionaire today is almost 60 years old, and at least a third of them are over 65. It is this generation that is now preparing to pass on its accumulated wealth to its children—the baby boom generation—defined as people born from 1946 to 1964. Inevitably, a central aspect of this wealth transfer will be whether and how much of it will be donated and to whom.

This impending wealth transfer doesn't just involve the Palm Beach set, because a substantial portion of it will pass to future generations in quite modest amounts. Economist Avery projected that, while 10 percent of the heirs will receive about two-thirds of the wealth, the rest will be distributed among the remaining 90 percent. The philanthropic impulses of this latter group will be proportionately modest as well, but if the past is any guide they will be equally as real. The implication for donors is that they will have to understand more about the options available to them than ever before. The implication for charities is that they had better do the same—and that they need to start planning to be a part of this transfer right away if they haven't already.

One useful starting point for both parties is to draw a thick black line at $675,000. As of this writing, this is the point at which both wealth transfer and charitable giving enjoy multiple options because inheritances over this amount are subject to the federal estate tax and various tax reduction strategies can interact with charitable giving. Additionally, there are different psychological and social implications for individuals and families contemplating philanthropic involvement (as of this writing, this tax was facing its first serious attack and many observers were predicting its eventual demise).

High net worth donors have a variety of options available to them that will further their goals. The key is to act early in order to avoid the less favorable tax consequences of outright gifts. Some vehicles include:

Gifts of appreciated property. Generally it is preferable for donors to give gifts of appreciated property directly to a charity rather than converting it to cash, paying the capital gains tax, and then donating the proceeds. Recent tax law reforms have broadened this opportunity after years of restrictions and many observers expect to see more such donations in the future. Donors must plan appreciated property donations carefully, however, since they cause one to be subject to the alternative minimum tax.

Charitable remainder trusts. Charitable remainder trusts allow donors (or someone else) to receive income from property while arranging for a charity to be the ultimate recipient of the property after the trust expires. Donors can take deductions based on the present value of the property, and there are several other benefits as well.

Private foundations. These vehicles are what one observer has called the status symbol of the new century as information age millionaires proliferate. Private foundations offer donors the opportunity to carefully target and control use of the donated property in a philanthropic venture. These benefits are balanced by greater reporting requirements, certain tax liabilities, and less advantageous treatment of property donations, so donors must carefully weigh the entire question before establishing a private foundation.

Community foundations. For some donors, community foundations can be an alternative to private foundations. Community foundations are public charities that receive contributions from a large number of individuals, often including the proceeds from terminated private foundations. There are administrative advantages to a community foundation, in addition to the fact that funds can still be targeted to specific purposes.

What about the rest of these likely heirs, the ones expecting to receive something less than the high six figures but who also want to donate intelligently? Actually, many of the same options listed above are also practical for this vast majority of baby boomer legatees. For example, gifts of appreciated property can offer the same value to charities no matter what the tax bracket of the donor happens to be, while allowing the donor tax advantages. Donations to community foundations are also advantageous and practical for inheritors of lesser wealth and will provide nearly the same benefits of control and efficiency.

Donor-Advised Funds: New Kids Change the Block

Various lists of the top ten fundraising organizations around the country recently reached a surprising milestone. On the *Nonprofit Times'* list of the top ten fundraisers—otherwise populated with venerable old agencies such as the Salvation Army (born in 1865), the American Red Cross (1881), and the YMCA (1851)—sits a very new entrant: Fidelity Charitable Gifts Fund, a virtual baby born in 1992.

Yes, that's Fidelity, as in the Boston-based investment powerhouse. Their Charitable Gifts Fund recently notched almost $600 million in yearly fundraising. This relatively late entrant into the annual fundraising derby didn't even exist when the last decade began. So how did the fund climb into such exclusive company so quickly?

The answer is partly that the Fidelity Charitable Gifts Fund isn't a service-providing, fundraising nonprofit at all, but rather a donor-advised giving mechanism. Unlike contributions to a nonprofit charity that provides a direct service and which uses donations directly, Fidelity's fund and others like it are simply a way for donors to make contributions to the charity of their choice. With the right size donation, any donor can essentially open his or her own miniature private foundation.

Critics deride this development as "checkbook charity" (a curious phrase—where else does charity come from?). Community foundations in particular were concerned about the effect it would have on their type of organization, and many fundraisers watched the brash upstarts surge ahead with a mixture of fear and envy. After all, planned giving advisors and groups such as the United Way's Tocqueville Givers program have long targeted precisely the same level of giver. But Fidelity's success has been notable.

Whatever else is true about the new donor options, one thing is clear—they are going to be around for a long time. Plus, new entrants are arising constantly. In addition to Fidelity, Vanguard has a fund, and Charles Schwab & Company just launched one too. In combination with Guidestar.org which offers online financial information on all public charities in the country, the new funds offer a new twist on a very old game.

The potential impact on nonprofits heavily dependent on traditional philanthropy is obvious. But why should the combination of popular donor-advised funds and ready access to financial information interest nonprofits that do little or no fundraising? The answer is that this new player is likely to have a widespread impact on the sector. Call it the philanthropic equivalent of managed care; it will set many of the standards and settle many of the debates even if it only directly affects a minority of the participants. There are some who say that even including donor-advised funds in the list of top fundraisers isn't fair because it's like comparing apples with oranges. True, they probably do represent a bushel of apples in a truckload of oranges. But the reason they must be acknowledged is because they will change the rules.

ELEMENTS OF A RESPONSE

Donor-advised funds are all about donor empowerment. As the concentration of management infrastructure moves from a select few hands such as workplaces to anyone who can click a mouse, the power of individual donors will grow. Nonprofits competing in the fundraising arena will need to keep a few things in mind to respond to the new balance of power. How they weave together a strategy depends on a great many variables, but here are some of the likely elements.

MAKE IT EASY

Many fundraisers today violate a cardinal rule of basic consumer marketing tactics—they make it downright difficult for donors to donate. The United Way is notorious for running administratively cumbersome, paper-based campaigns that unfold with excruciating sameness each year. Special events organizers design massive fundraisers in locations with poor parking. Planned giving specialists don't return phone calls, and so on.

Rather than unwittingly erecting barriers against potential donors, nonprofits must learn how to go out of their way to lower them. Convenience and timesaving are two of the most compelling drivers of innovation in today's economy. Cell phones are more convenient and take less time than finding a pay phone. Broadband Internet connections get us to the same place as dial-up services, but are much faster. Faxes are more convenient than sending packages through the mail, and so forth.

Fundraisers must find ways to make it far easier for donors to donate than ever before. Don't have cash? We accept credit cards. Can't figure out whether you should donate cash or stocks? Step right over here and speak with our planned giving counselor. Want to know about the quality of our services? Here's a one-page summary and a handful of testimonials from our former consumers; would you like to meet some of the staff? Making the task of donating much easier is almost a total shift in the model that many are using right now.

LOWER ADMINISTRATIVE COSTS

Other than mission, services, and ease of use the major consumer appeal in donor-advised funds is going to be low administrative costs. It's not fair to put so much emphasis on low administrative costs, it's not smart in the long run, and it isn't terribly helpful—but donors love it. This is likely to be the deepest and most profound effect of making charities' financial information and donor options widely available online. Comparative analysis among charities will be easier than ever, and many donors and their advisors are certain to take the time to do it. Donors want to feel that their money is going to efficient nonprofits without large overhead costs, and the ready availability of this information will cement that behavior.

Two things will come from this dynamic. First, a low overhead rate will probably become the gold standard of nonprofit operations. This will put pressure on nonprofits to issue accurate IRS Form 990s, which is the basis of the Guidestar database. The form will go from being an informational return to an important element of fundraising strategy.

The second result is that even organizations that do little or no fundraising will feel some spillover pressure to keep administrative costs low. Reporters, analysts, grant evaluators, and ordinary donors will encourage the already present sentiment against administrative spending. The quest for reported efficiency will be muted but strong.

THE IMPORTANCE OF BRANDING

For donors, the flip side to empowerment is unlimited choice. If a donor decides to donate assets to charity without having a particular organization in mind, how will he or she decide which agency to choose? There are about 700,000 public charities in this country. If picking a mutual fund out of a population of a few thousand sometimes seems mind-boggling, imagine how hard it will be for donors to zero in on the charity of their choice.

In time, donors' most reliable guide to the right recipient agencies is likely to be the same thing that helps simplify choices in the grocery store—brand names. Nonprofits that have a recognizable "brand"—whether it's from being part of a national system or just good local visibility—will have a distinct advantage. While local affiliates of national systems will obviously have an edge in the name recognition department, there is plenty of room for freestanding nonprofits to create their own intensely local following.

THE NEED TO BE TECHNOLOGY SAVVY

Recently we were at a planning session for a statewide group of government-funded nonprofits at which multimillion dollar annual investments in technology were discussed as a priority second only to upgrading direct care workers' salaries. This reflects how dominant technology is becoming even in the largely nontechnological nonprofit environment.

Although it may be a bit of a stretch, many nonprofit managers are learning to value technology in more areas than just the business office. A handy rule of thumb is that technology will change activities involving money faster than any other area, which is why online fundraising is such a natural extension of the efficiencies that computers have produced in accounting and finance over the years.

The challenge for fundraisers is to learn to figuratively move the computers from the accounting office into development activities. Ironically, this will necessitate getting much more technologically savvy around other areas such as service reporting, since empowered donors will naturally want to know that they are getting the maximum effectiveness for their donation.

BECOMING RESEARCHERS

Finally, empowered and knowledgeable donors demand empowered and knowledgeable recipients. If donors will get to know more about their beneficiaries, their beneficiaries will have to know even more about the case for their own organizations. This is truly a marketing and fund development skill, but it is not one which all nonprofits have in-house. To carve out a distinctive niche, however, nonprofits will have to learn how to use the same information that their donors are using.

Donor-advised funds are going to change the rules. It's not hard to imagine a future in which most of the 10 largest fundraisers are not direct service providers like the Red Cross or the YMCA but are donor-advised funds. When that happens streetsmart nonprofit managers will know how to respond—and they'll probably make a few new rules of their own in the process.

Index